100 SUCCESSFUL
COLLEGE
APPLICATION
ESSAYS

100 SUCCESSFUL
COLLEGE
APPLICATION
ESSAYS

THIRD EDITION

COMPILED AND EDITED BY
MEMBERS OF THE STAFF OF
The Harvard Independent

 NEW AMERICAN LIBRARY

New American Library
Published by the Penguin Group
Penguin Group (USA) Inc., 375 Hudson Street,
New York, New York 10014, USA

USA | Canada | UK | Ireland | Australia | New Zealand | India | South Africa | China

Penguin Books Ltd., Registered Offices: 80 Strand, London WC2R 0RL, England
For more information about the Penguin Group visit penguin.com.

Published by New American Library, a division of Penguin Group (USA) Inc. Previously
published in a Plume edition.

First Printing (Third Edition), July 2013

NAL REGISTERED TRADEMARK—MARCA REGISTRADA

NEW AMERICAN LIBRARY TRADE PAPERBACK ISBN: 978-0-451-41761-9

Printed in the United States of America
10 9 8 7

PUBLISHER'S NOTE
While the author has made every effort to provide accurate telephone numbers, Internet
addresses and other contact information at the time of publication, neither the publisher nor the
author assumes any responsibility for errors, or for changes that occur after publication. Further,
publisher does not have any control over and does not assume any responsibility for author or
third-party Web sites or their content.

To Dr. Nicholas T. Macris

*—who, like the essays in this book,
inspires by way of example*

ACKNOWLEDGMENTS

We would like to thank many people. First, the hundreds of students who submitted their essays for consideration. Their help, with only the knowledge that their experience might benefit others in return, has been invaluable.

Our appreciation, as always, to Thomas Harvey, for his wise advice, his experience, and his introduction.

Often support comes from a place where it is least expected. Thanks to the partnership of Schafe, Sean, and Now, who now know the true meaning of good jobs at good wages. Thanks also to Mike for providing an opportunity.

Special appreciation to Martha Dustin, for her General Attitude and her reading skills, to our sister Stephanie, who promised that all her friends' children would buy a copy, and to Mary Beth Whitson for always knowing when to break for coffee.

Most of all, we'd like to thank our parents.

And, of course, special thanks to George Bear.

The following editors selected the 100 essays in this book from the hundreds of pieces submitted. Editors-in-chief: Christopher J. Georges (Executive Editor of the *Harvard Crimson*, 1987); Gigi E. Georges (Managing Editor of the *Wellesley News*, 1988); Managing Editor: Shari Rudavsky (Managing Editor of the *Harvard Crimson*, 1988).

Editorial Staff: Keith O. Boykin (Editor-in-chief and Chairman of the *Dartmouth News*, 1987); Sean Dobson (writer for the *Yale Daily News*, 1987); Martha Dustin (staff editor of the *Harvard Independent*

Insider's Guide to Prep Schools, 1987); Tony Laden (President of the *Harvard Independent,* 1988); David Lee (President of the *Harvard Independent,* 1987); Kevin Park (Publisher of the *Harvard Independent,* 1988); John R. Schafer (Coeditor-in-chief of *The Williams Record,* 1987); Wade Roush (Editor-in-chief of the *Harvard Independent,* 1988).

Thanks to the following staff members for their work on the second edition: Alexander P. Nyren, Alicia Llosa, Karen Kiang, and Will Reckler.

Finally, thanks to Gary Gerbrant and Whitney Lee for their efforts in putting together this third edition.

The following people provided the comments and remarks that follow the essays: Natalie Aharonian, former Director of Admission, Wellesley College, Wellesley, MA; Brenda Lee Barr, MSEd., College Counselor, Randolph-Macon Academy, Front Royal, VA; Stanley A. Bosworth, Headmaster, Saint Ann's School, Brooklyn, NY; Ann A. Frietas, College Counselor, Bellarmine College Prep, San Jose, CA; Ted Grabowski, Director of Guidance, Holy Ghost Prep, Bensalem, PA; Amy Miller Harriman, Admissions Director, Randolph-Macon Academy, Front Royal, VA; Tom D. Harvey, former Assistant Headmaster for External Affairs, Poly Prep Country Day School, Brooklyn, NY; Michael A. Hricko, Provincial Assistant for Secondary and Presecondary Education, Maryland Province Jesuits, Baltimore, MD; Robert Koppert, Director of College Counseling, The Dalton School, New York, NY; John McClintoch, former College Counselor, Francis W. Parker School, Chicago, IL; John C. Merrill, III, Director of College Counseling, The Pingree School, South Hamilton, MA; Robert C. Miller, College Counselor, Happy Valley School, Ojai, CA; John W. Mudge, College Advisor, Garrison Forest School, Garrison, MD; Richard J. O'Hara, The Head of the School, The Wellington School, Columbus, OH; Maxine Rodberg, Director of the Writing Center and Senior Preceptor in Expository Writing, Harvard University, Cambridge, MA; Bryan P. Seese, former

Director of Placement, Milton Hershey School, Hershey, PA; Peter Taubman, Graduate Deputy for the School of Education and Head of Adolescent Education, Brooklyn College, Brooklyn, NY; Hal D. Tayloe, former Chairman, English Dept., Hampton Roads Academy, Newport News, VA; Arthur S. Thomas, Director of College Counseling, The Lawrenceville School, Lawrenceville, NJ.

CONTENTS

100 SUCCESSFUL
COLLEGE
APPLICATION
ESSAYS

PREFACE

It's early January. College applications are due in 48 hours, and your applications are complete—except for the essay.

Why not? Perhaps you fear writing something that will not match the record displayed throughout the rest of the application. Perhaps because of the difficulty of capturing your personality on a single sheet of paper. Or maybe you still are waiting for an original idea—something that will prompt the admissions officers to place your application in their "great thinkers of the 21st century" folder.

You call a friend. "... Oh, you've already finished your essay," you say. "Me? Oh, I'm almost there. Just have to finish thinking of a topic. ... What did you write about? ... No kidding. The electoral college. Nice choice. ..."

You want to say something about *yourself,* but you don't want to sound pretentious. You want to show them you're different—better even—than the next applicant, and you want to show it on a single sheet of paper. You want to show them you're funny, or creative, or bright, or athletic, or ambitious. You want to let them know that you deserve to go to *their* college.

The intent of this book is not to give advice. Nor is it a how-to guide. Instead, it is intended to inspire by way of example.

With that said, we will now offer three bits of somewhat ambiguous advice—which we hope the rest of this book serves to illustrate:

First, try not to accomplish too much in your essay. Less is more.

Second, poor essays make a big deal out of nothing (e.g., learn to respect mankind from serving as captain of JV basketball), and successful essays take respectable accomplishment and keep it in perspective.

Finally, be loose. This doesn't mean writing a string of jokes. On the other hand, write for admissions officers, not for the law review. Keep it simple, easy to follow, and "be what thou art"—a high school student.

Throughout this book, we have attempted to illustrate that a successful college application essay need not be produced by a gifted writer—otherwise this would be a very short book. We could not, of course, resist including a number of essays written by talented writers; however, we also strove more to include essays that stood out for other reasons. And these, we believe, deserve greater attention simply because they illustrate what can be done with a little creativity and a little thought. And that, more than anything, may be what separates the average essay from the successful one.

After almost every essay, you'll find a "Comment" written by one of the professional admissions officers or counselors who helped us with our selections. In the text, they are identified by their initials; their full names can be found on page viii–ix.

The essays in this book are those that college and high school officials as well as the editors of this book have selected as outstanding, successful, unusual, or exceptionally thoughtful. The purpose of the book is simply to expose students to various techniques in essay writing and to illustrate that there is no one type of essay that should or should not be written.

—THE EDITORS

ON WRITING THE COLLEGE ESSAY

Simplicity and Impact

Engaging a tired, often-bored admissions officer's interest is a difficult task, but it doesn't require Shakespearean talents. What it does need, though, is a unique approach. After reading that first sentence can you guess the topic of the essay? Or are you left without a clue? When writing an application essay, a reader's concentration is held by consistent and logical flow. While an admissions essay doesn't have to spell things out for the reader, it needs to tell the reader something interesting and unique, and once you have done that, you have satisfied the first condition in how to write an admissions essay. Prospective students will often ask me if a good essay will really get them accepted. The truth is that while no essay will make an unqualified student acceptable, a good essay can help a qualified applicant stand out from the competition. A good essay just might be what turns a "maybe" into a "yes."

The college application process takes time, preparation and creativity, which is a lot for any active senior to handle. I suggest using the summer before your senior year to craft your essay. While there is no magic formula for the perfect admission essay, there are a few things prospective college students should know. Write about yourself. A great history paper might be very well written, but it doesn't tell me anything about the writer. Regardless of the topic, make sure you shine through your essay. Use your own voice. Admissions officers can tell the difference between the voice of a forty-year-old professor and a high school senior. Be genuine. Don't try to impress me, because I've heard it all. Just tell me what is important to you. Here are a few do's and don'ts to help guide you through the writing process:

- Consider a simple topic. Sometimes it's the simple things in life that make the best essays. Some of my favorites have included essays that reflect on the daily subway ride to school, or what the family goldfish observed from the fishbowl perched on the family kitchen table. It doesn't have to be a life-changing event to be interesting and informative.

- Don't be afraid to be humorous (within reason). If you are a naturally funny person, let that shine through! I like essays that have sentiment and humor and read like a student wrote it from their heart.

- Share your opinions, but avoid anything too risky or controversial. Your essay will be read by a diverse group of individuals from a wide range of backgrounds, so try to appeal to the broadest audience possible.

- Tell a good story. Show me why you are compassionate; don't tell me you are. Show me that you have overcome great difficulty; don't start your essay with "I have overcome great difficulties."

- Don't repeat what is already in your application. If you go to a performing arts school and all of your extracurricular activities and awards relate to dance, don't write about how much you love dancing. Tell me something I couldn't know just from reading the other parts of your application.

—AMY MILLER HARRIMAN
Admissions Director, Randolph-Macon Academy
Front Royal, VA

You Will Like Me

You will like me. It's the selling point of writing every college admissions essay. When tasked with composing my own for a master's program, I was stymied. What to write about? How to have an edited, coherent and authentic writing piece possessing punch and pizzazz, showcasing my personality in a mere five hundred words? In my college-counseling career, I had assisted roughly four hundred students on their very own essays. However, at this time, I was on the other side of the desk. My blank mind bounced around the room. The only conclusion I reached was that bungee jumping carries less anxiety than the cursor mocking me with its rhythmic vertical blink. Now I was the frustrated student wanting someone to like me through my words.

As the panic began to build, I assessed the situation. The deadline was thankfully far removed, giving plenty of opportunity for rewriting. "The only good writing is rewriting" was my mantra when working with students. Check that box. Next was the hard one: What on earth to write about? How to put one's soul on a piece of paper?

For a counselor, coaxing an essay out of a student involves trust. Students are sharing the most intimate details of their lives, some which have not ever seen daylight. All have a common goal: To stand out and shout, "Hey, you up there, pick me!" Writing the college essay takes immense patience and a belief in yourself. It involves quelling tears, boosting confidence and using an objective overview.

The essay itself breaks the paradigm of writing as students know it. The traditional structured, formulaic approach of storytelling involves a clear introduction, followed by details that slide into a neatly wrapped conclusion. Writing for college essays shakes up the entire process, as the conclusion must now be the introduction. An attention-grabbing first sentence captures the reader and begs him or her not to put down the essay. These openers can be incredibly descriptive: "Looking forward we stand, together, like monoliths in the morning sun." They can allude to conflict: "As I stepped out of my room, I heard him shout, 'Freeze!'" Or simply lean toward the wistful loss of childhood: "I was eight years old when I found out Santa wasn't real." Each opener holds the common promise of knowing more about the flesh behind the grades and the test scores.

A successful essay employs all five senses, which assist in opening the channels of communication. With lines like "the bugle crying out reveille" or "being faced with a tall dark form looming above me" or "slowly tiptoeing toward the stairs wondering what I would see next," the reader is thrust into the story, still wanting to read despite already knowing the conclusion.

Thus I was returned to the task, the dreaded essay. I had utilized all I had taught students, yet something was amiss. My head nodding forward, I came to the realization that my fears were tangible, and the wonderful happened. For me to have trepidation meant I had a true connection. The aha moment that cannot be taught is an emotional link to what you choose to write about. Suddenly, clarity befell my thoughts, and I recognized as my students before me: I am the owner of this essay. You will like me.

—BRENDA LEE BARR, MSEd.
College Counselor, Randolph-Macon Academy
Front Royal, VA

Advice from the Inside

Someone once calculated that I have read around two hundred thousand applications for admission, give or take a couple thousand, since becoming an admissions dean. Does that make me an expert on the subject of admissions essays? Nope. Does it qualify me to offer a few observations about such essays, based on my experience? Maybe. The editors apparently think so. I promised I'd give it a try.

The essay is the main life-support system of the application. Let's face it, most of a college application is a matter of filling in the blank spaces, listing things. Listing your accomplishments and interests, neatly listing them, sometimes even imaginatively listing them, but listing them nevertheless. Takes about a half hour at the outside. The essay is the applicant's opportunity to breathe some life into the folder, to remind the reader that all of those numbers and letter grades and adjectives and test scores and lists of activities represent, for better or for worse, yet another and different person out there.

When I was an admissions dean and faced the task early each January of reading through some fifteen thousand or so applications, I must confess that I was not thrilled at the prospect of seeing just how many different ways in which the number of varsity letters, or the number of years in the orchestra, or the number of offices held could be expressed. Even the recommendations from teachers and counselors, which, when well done, can bring a candidate to life, frequently fall short of doing so, resorting as they almost invariably must to a rather limited set of adjectives (even the superlatives become routine) to limn the students about whom they are writing. It was the essays I looked forward to, not to give a thumbs-up or thumbs-down to an applicant, but rather simply to help give a particular shape or outline to the person who garnered the grades and test scores and awards and superlative adjectives I read about in the rest of the folder.

In an age of McRankings and media hype about "hot colleges," there is unfortunately a lemminglike tendency of students with similar abilities and accomplishments to cluster their applications at an unreasonably (or so it seems to me) limited number of particular colleges and universities. The result, alas, is that the range among applicants along any one of these numerical/adjectival dimensions above is, at many colleges, often very narrow. A reader of applications at such colleges can become positively glassy-eyed after the first five hundred or so. More often than not, it is the more personal nature of the essays that breaks the monotony and engages the reader.

Keep in mind that a college application is a set of six or seven hooks, on four or five of which most candidates for admissions are going to hang their hats. The essay is only one such hook. Save for those few instances in which candidates wrote essays so completely lacking in taste as to make us marvel at the fact that they even had bothered to apply, in my experience no one was ever admitted *solely* on the basis of a great essay and no one was ever denied admission *solely* on the basis of a poor essay. (See below on "fit.")

Also keep in mind that good essay topics or questions are often as difficult for the colleges to think up as they are for the applicants to respond to. (Not much solace there, I admit.) Unlike "test" questions, they're not set to elicit (or even to imply) right or wrong answers. Ideally, they simply provide some fertile ground to be plowed by applicants from all sorts of backgrounds and with quite different interests and experiences, while at the same time keeping the area sufficiently fenced in so as to allow for comparability. In some instances, essay topics simply reflect the preferences of those who have to read them. My own preference, for instance, was for questions that I hoped would be fun to answer and that I also hoped would elicit answers fun to read. These are some of the reasons why essay topics not only vary enormously from college to college, but even year to year at the same college. The essay is the one part of the application that allows a student to think out loud. Indeed, when you stop to think about it, it's the only part of the application that usually requires any thinking at all!

Since most readers of application essays (myself included) are not by any stretch of the imagination experts in that particular art form, and indeed frequently disagree among themselves over the merits of one or another essay, my first piece of advice is to write your essays, *not* for some imaginary admissions officer or faculty member at the other end, but for yourselves, or for a favorite avuncular relative, or roommate. Write it for anyone *other* than that admissions person whom you've come to convince yourself holds your life in his or her hands. (I read somewhere that the term "short shrift" originally referred to a brief respite for confession before execution. Don't consider your essay "short shrift." Relax.)

That brings me to my second piece of advice. When you write your essay, consider simply telling a story. I can think of few college application essay topics, including the weightiest, that don't provide the student with an opportunity to tell a story. I'm convinced that storytelling comes more naturally to most of us, and also more accurately expresses our nature, than does essay writing. Ask me to tell a story, no problem. Ask me to write an essay and I break out in a sweat. But I long ago figured out that some of the best essays I've ever read are simply stories well told.

Besides, stories need not be long to be effective, a not inconsequential virtue, given that colleges frequently require that an essay be no longer than a single page. Don't consider brevity a limitation. You should be able to tell a story in just one page. It has always struck me that a poem is a really *short* "short story." The art of poetry is in knowing what to leave out. What is left out is often precisely what draws the reader in. That's as true for storytellers as for poets. And what you want to do is draw in the reader of your application. Don't hesitate to risk leaving something to the reader's imagination. (Here I must confess that no matter what kind of writing I'm doing, I try to discipline myself to go back over it and remove the unnecessary baggage that always creeps in, an exercise delightfully taught in William Zinsser's *On Writing Well*.)

My third piece of advice is to invest some time in reading some good writing before sitting down to write your own essay. I find I *have* to do that. I think most of us have a passive vocabulary and even ways of expressing ourselves that are far more intricate and colorful and imaginative than that we're normally required to draw upon to get through an average day. Reading a good book or a good essay can sometimes ignite the same skills in the reader. You probably have your own favorites. Mine include people like E. B. White, Robertson Davies, Stephen Jay Gould, Russell Baker, John McPhee, Joseph Epstein, Garrison Keillor, and Red Smith, to name a few. Good writing is contagious. It can also put you in an appropriate frame of mind for embarking on your essay. Observe how they tell a story. Observe how they tell a story in order to make a point. Observe how they draw the reader in, often from the first sentence. Keep in mind also that there's nothing wrong with imitating a good writer. That is how many writers we now consider "good" started out.

My fourth piece of advice is to be sure that your essay reflects you, and not some idealized version of yourself that you have come to imagine is precisely the kind of person an admissions office will be most favorably disposed toward. In my most plaintive moments as an admissions dean, I could be heard stalking the office corridors shouting, "Where in the hell are the Huckleberry Finns?" Such explosions normally took place after I'd made my way through a long string of applications that left me convinced we had cornered the market on saints and scholars, none of whom had ever stumbled, faltered, or failed at anything, and few of whom seemed real. To a certain extent, the entire admissions process invites that. Applicants are constantly advised to "put their best foot forward." But I must confess that I always liked the ones who put *both* feet forward. Whatever number of feet you plan to put forward or to stand on, make sure that your essay "fits" your application.

An application where the various pieces don't appear to "fit" together stands out like a sore thumb. As with admissions officers, students come in all shapes and sizes, with different personalities and ways of approaching the world. Some are gregarious; some are shy. Some are athletically inclined, and some are more sedentary. Some are more mature in some aspects of their lives than in others. The freshman class at any college in the country will be made up of students who exhibit a mix of all of these traits and many more. What throws off a reader of an application is a sharp and inexplicable contrast between a student's essay and everything that that reader has learned about the student throughout the rest of the application. For instance, an essay that is so highly polished that even a tenured professor would be proud to submit it for publication, from an applicant whom a reader otherwise finds attractive precisely because the evidence throughout the rest of the folder depicts a diamond in the rough, naturally raises questions in the reader's mind about whether the essay is really the work of the student. How does one square this brilliantly put essay, not only with comments from the applicant's teachers that poor writing skills constitute his only major weakness, but also with the student's rather modest writing skills that are all too evident throughout the rest of the application?

This is not to say that, if you need to, you should not have someone else whose judgment you value take a look at your essay in order to point out typos, grammatical errors, or even, ahem, incomprehensibility. But I can't emphasize enough (well, maybe I can) that the style, flavor, and substance of your essay needs to *be* your own and to *look* your own and to *sound* like you. In a word, your essay (in fact, your entire application) should *smell* authentic.

I guess what I am saying here is that essays that appear contrived, either in style or substance, often stand out and can end up working against an otherwise attractive applicant. My hunch is that many students tend to underestimate their attractiveness compared with other applicants, come to imagine (erroneously) that colleges have some single, ideal admissions candidate in mind, and in the course of trying to come off as this imagined "ideal" candidate actually do themselves a disservice in the process. (With only a slight amount of exaggeration involved, the applicant I remember most quickly putting in the "admit" pile was one who wrote: "As you will notice, my test scores are quite low. They are accurate.")

My fifth piece of advice is not to ask of your essay that it carry too heavy a load. Don't use the essay to drop names, or to remind the reader that your parents are alumni of the college, or to rationalize a low grade or a low test score or a lost election of yearbook editor. Essays that are used to tell a college everything you think they should know about you but didn't ask elsewhere in the application come to resemble junk sculptures. Just give the essay question or topic itself your best shot. (If there *is* additional information or an explanation you think is useful for the college to have in considering your application, simply add an extra sheet and attach it to your application papers.)

Also, resist the temptation to write the *all-purpose* essay, to which you then make small adjustments in order to use it for all of your college applications no matter how different the essay questions or topics they set before you. Such essays are painfully obvious, and more often than not engender a negative reaction. Just as applicants want to be treated as individuals by each of the colleges to which they are applying, so, too, do the colleges desire that their applications be treated individually by the applicants. At least that's the way we feel.

My last piece of advice is to tell you to sort and sift any advice you receive (including my own) and to settle only on that which intuitively makes sense to you. As crazy and as varied as the admissions process seems when you are going through it, it's always struck me that one of the virtues of admission to American colleges and universities is precisely the lack of a consensus among even the most selective colleges on what the "perfect" application looks like or who the most desirable applicants are. The observations I've made here are based upon my particular experience in reading the applications at one college and one university over a twenty-year period. They're not offered from on high, but rather simply on the off chance that one or another of them just might ring a bell with you. Whatever, good luck.

—FRED A. HARGADON
Former Dean of Admission,
Princeton University
Princeton, NJ

(Fred A. Hargadon was Dean of Admissions at Swarthmore College from 1964 to 1969, and Dean of Admission at Stanford University from 1969 to 1984.)

How to Use This Book

You will find this book useful if you use it well, but you will not find a formula for success here. The essays included are as varied as the people who wrote them. Some are long. Some are short. Some are deeply moving. Some are hilariously irreverent. Some are profoundly personal and some are wonderfully whimsical. Yet they are all judged effective, or successful.

The message here is a simple one. Be honest and be confident. Be willing to be different by being yourself. Those who read your essays will be looking for reasons to like you. Trust them by writing what you feel, and by writing whatever you feel.

Take chances. If you think you can be funny, be funny. If you think you have a particular skill or personal quality worthy of note, send the message. This is not the time to be cautious.

Your essay will succeed, if you are prepared when you write it.

As you read the essays here, conduct an experiment. Pick out the ones you like best, and then reexamine their openings. You will find that the best essays have the best openings. A good opening is the result of forethought. If you know what you want to write, and you find an effective way to begin, the essay will pour out of your pencil.

—THOMAS D. HARVEY
Former Assistant Headmaster for External Affairs,
Poly Prep Country Day School,
Brooklyn, NY

ESSAYS ON APPLYING TO COLLEGE

Charles W. Applegate
College: Ohio Wesleyan University

Here I sit, my pen vying for equal time in my hand as some Connecticut School of Broadcasting flunkie blabbers on and on and my glass of Diet Coke wordlessly whispers of its passage from fizzy to flat. "What am I, Sam?" I beseech of my cat, who is disdainfully picking over the remains of his Tuna Entree and eyeing the purposeful plummeting of the sky's best snowflakes with the vigorous venom of a cat grown old enough to truly despise winter.

"Ahh," he hisses, lidded eyes coming to bear on my vaguely despondent figure. "You are, oh Grasshopper, what you accomplish. A man (or, in your case, a boy) can only be measured by his achievements."

"Sam, I'd buy it if you were a Siamese, but let's face it. You're a Domestic Shorthair rescued by me from a West Side alley in New York. Now come on. I need this for my Beloit essay."

"Okay, Charles. You want to know what you are? You are an insignificant eighteen-year-old kid pretending to be an adult, trying to write about some aspect of your rather short life and make it seem not only interesting, but significant, too. No offense, but the best thing you ever did in your life was to adopt me."

"That's not quite true, Sam, but you do have a point." Sam disdainfully shook his left front paw and resumed glowering at the snowflakes' gently offensive descent.

Snowflakes notwithstanding (for I in my youth still enjoy them greatly), my snide little fur-face is right. As my pen hand evicts my head and my pen begins to romp across the paper, I look back on my life and find a notable paucity of great achievements and memorable experiences. I see, complete with warm feelings of triumph and heightened self-esteem, the earning of my driver's license, my first date, my first (and only) sack in a football game, and other memorabilia of my not-so-distant youth. Not to say that I've had an uneventful life, but there isn't too much to brag about.

This is where what Sam just said comes into play. One simple word which explains my aforementioned paucity of experience. That word, if you have not already guessed it, is eighteen. After all, I've been on this earth for but one-quarter of my expected life span, and it's only in the past few years that I have gained leave to explore the world's virginal vistas, so it's no surprise to me that my past is far from chock-full of wondrous life experiences.

Picture if you will the world reduced to the comparative microcosm of a chicken coop, perhaps with Sam playing a role as the Grim Reaper, or the threat of Communism, or the Fuller Brush salesman, or some other such menacing apparition. Following through with the analogy, I have been spending my time in the eggshell of high school. I am soon due to be released into the training ground of the coop's floor, which serves as a college designed to prepare me for the dangers, inconsistencies, and complexities of the adult world outside the barnyard.

While the snowflakes remorselessly mount their attack against my poor, aged cat, I ponder the infinite mysteries of college. Why college? Sam is remarkably uncommunicative, his ears flattened with rage at the sky's vile behavior, and refuses to answer my query.

Sitting here in the kitchen, all the wrong reasons for college are readily apparent, and I chant aloud of money, power, prestige, and the endless others that send people scurrying to the shelter of higher education in the hope that one will show some sign of earning my feline mentor's stamp of approval. Nothing. He sits on the window like a stone meatloaf. Glumly, I stare into the oven, my wave of inspiration having crested and broken on the beach of writer's block.

Now, though, I feel as if I'm being watched. Slowly, I turn to the window and gaze into two deep, burning liquid eyes. Sam has abandoned his snowflakes for my problem.

"You never could see the forest for the trees, could you? What is it that you were complaining about earlier? A lack of experience, wasn't it? Now then, tell me what college is for."

As the words sinuously roll off his tongue, I realize how totally correct he is. I need college to learn, not how to read or add, but how to live.

College is the beginning of real life, of life outside the chicken coop. And it is where I will begin my life.

Jennifer Applegate
College: University of Pennsylvania

MELPOMENE STRIKES

"I don't know yet," she replied. "I'd like to write a poem, since I think that's my forte, but I just can't find the inspiration under this kind of pressure."

"I think I can help you," Martha said slowly. "Call this number and ask for Calliope," she said as she scribbled. "Gotta run."

That night the girl sat for a full hour staring at the blank sheet of 8½" x 11" paper before she dug out the bubblegum wrapper and dialed the number etched on it in #2 pencil. After three rings there was a short silence and a perky voice chirped, "Calliope and Company, may I help you?"

"Uh, yes," the girl stammered. "May I speak with Calliope, please?"

"Calliope is in a board meeting right now," the voice bubbled. "May I connect you with another party?"

"I don't really know," the girl replied, flustered. "I was told to ask for Calliope, but if there's someone covering for her . . ."

"Well, let's see . . ." Sounds of pages flipping. "I believe Erato and Thalia are free, but I can't be sure. What is it you would like to write?"

"Um, a poem," she replied, puzzled.

"Wellllll," the voice said, "Calliope deals with overall eloquence, but perhaps Erato could help you. Is this a . . . love poem?"

Is it? the girl wondered furtively. "No, not really."

"Hmmmm . . . Perhaps bucolic poetry? Thalia is free today."

"No, that's not quite right somehow . . . I don't suppose you have a resident expert on prose poetry, do you?"

There was a tinkling laugh. "No, I'm afraid not. Would you like to try your hand at music or dance? I could ring up Euterpe or Terpsichore for you."

Where do they get these names, she smiled to herself. "No, I'm afraid this has to be visual. It has to be done on one sheet of paper."

There was a puzzled silence. "Oh . . . I see. Can you use both sides?"

"Um, I'm not sure. Good question . . . lemme check."

She grabbed at the sheet and quickly scanned it. "'. . . on or with an 8½" x 11" piece of paper . . .' Yeah, I guess you can." She was growing desperate, staring at the list of deadlines posted above her desk. "I just need a little inspiration on this poem, that's all. It's very important."

"I could try for Polyhymnia . . . she's the muse of sacred lyric poetry."

"I said important, not sacred . . . did you say muse?"

"Well, of course," the voice bubbled. "You are speaking to Calliope and Company, Muses, an agency designed to help inspire artists of all sorts."

Where did Martha get this number, she wondered. Ready to try anything, she said dully, "Oh. Well, who can inspire me?"

"Well, I'm afraid I don't quite know what to suggest," the voice said sadly. "Please hold while I check with Calliope."

Blowing the stray hairs out of her eyes, the girl slumped back in her chair and sighed, listening with half an ear to the faint strains of lute Muzak. A frosty voice broke the tranquility, shattering her thoughts: "Calliope speaking," it snapped. "Is there a problem?"

"No, ma'am," the girl stammered. "I mean, yes, there is . . . I want to write a poem, and I need it by the first of the year."

"And what is it you wanted of us?"

"Inspiration?" she quavered.

"Of course," Calliope sneered witheringly. "May I ask why you need this so soon?"

"College essay," she replied in a near-whisper.

"For whom?"

"University of Pennsylvania."

"And the question is?"

"Um . . ." She grabbed once more at the sheet. "'. . . your sense of imagination and creativity are also important to us . . . Create something on or with an 8½" x 11" piece of paper or other thin, flat material. All means of expression, written or otherwise, are equally encouraged.'"

There was a dead silence on the other end of the line for a minute. Then Calliope, colder than ever, hissed, "You would do better to simply recopy and send a poem that you had already written. One that you created spontaneously, not under a royal command. One does not call upon a muse and order her to inspire. Inspiration does not come when one tries to force it. Do I make myself perfectly clear?"

The lightbulb clicked on over her head. "Oh! So that's why I had that mental block! It was the pressure . . . you know, normally I can just sit down and churn out some funny little story or a nice poem with some good images, but this 'Fill up this paper' business just threw me!"

"Wonderful," said Calliope, unenthused. "And now if you'll excuse me—"

"Wait!" the girl shrieked. "What about Penn?!?"

Calliope snarled. "Tell Penn that creativity can't be forced," she snapped. Click.

Buzzzzzzzzzzzzzzzzzzzzzzzzzzzzzzzzzzzzzzzzzzzzzzzzzzzz . . .

COMMENT:

Terrific! Organized confusion and a spoof on anyone not up on his mythology. The central figure asks, "Where do they get these names?" only shortly after the reader asks the same question. There is something dreamlike about the essay. It's very clever. (TH)

Eric A. Maki
College: Brown University

High above the Earth in a starship from the Andromeda Galaxy, two aliens stand gazing out a viewport at the brilliant blue orb below. They are intergalactic scouts, sent from the planet Nerfon to gather information on this strange civilization recently discovered by Nerfonian astronomers. Zilbub, a high-ranking military officer, has the task of gauging the Earth's military strength. Zarkon, a Nerfonian anthropologist, has been assigned to gather all possible information concerning Earth's culture . . .

"Well, Zarkon, my duties are nearly completed. It has been quite an easy task to monitor the military activities of the Earth creatures from here. But your task intrigues me. Just how do you propose to gather information regarding this strange and primitive culture?"

"I have decided that the best way to do this will be to replace an entrant into an Earth 'university' with one of our robotic spy clones. This action will provide us with unlimited acsess to a huge storehouse of information without causing any undue alarm among the Earthmen. Hopefully, they will never notice the switch."

"Am I to assume that you have already found a suitable candidate for replacement?"

"Yes, Zilbub. He is called Eric Maki, and is an applicant to the institute of higher learning the Earthlings call 'Brown University.'"

"Ah, yes . . . 'Brown' . . . I have heard the name mentioned in

Earthling transmissions. It would be quite an accomplishment to have one of our agents inside such a place. But are you sure this 'Eric Maki' will be admitted to Brown?"

"Well, Zilbub, we cannot be absolutely certain. The Earthlings who control the 'universities' employ other Earthlings, called 'admissions officers,' to determine such things. In my opinion, however, he seems a most promising candidate."

"Hmmm . . . what are the characteristics of this creature?"

"Physically, he is five and one-half Earth 'feet' tall. He will certainly never be a member of the association of giants the Earthlings call the 'National Basketball Association.' Fortunately, though, extreme height is not a requirement for entry into the place called 'Brown.'"

"Does the creature hold any position of importance among his fellow beings?"

"He is a leader among those of his age, holding a local position they call 'senior class president.'"

"Ah . . . a leader . . . he may be the kind of creature I can identify with . . . tell me, Zarkon—does he use his power to subjugate and conquer other Earthlings?"

"No, Zilbub, you misunderstand. His main function is to organize his fellow beings—'classmates,' to use the Earth term—in preparation for year-end ceremonies called 'the prom' and 'graduation.' He also serves as a representative of his 'class' in dealings with the older Earthlings known as 'school administrators.' He was elected to this position, rather than ready-grown in a test tube, as our leaders are back on Nerfon."

"This 'democratic process' by which they select their leaders is quite amusing to me. Besides, a leader without a military to enforce his decisions seems hopelessly powerless."

"Nevertheless, Zilbub, he is a representative of over one hundred fellow Earthmen. It is a position of great responsibility, even if he has no armies to command. He has, judging by many observations, performed his duties well."

"I am curious, Zarkon . . . as to how these Earth creatures select a leader such as this one; what qualities does this 'Eric Maki' possess which distinguish him from the others?"

"According to the data I have collected, he seems to be of above-average intelligence, doing well in his studies and on the 'Scholastic Aptitude Test,' a much-feared trial among the Earth creatures. Also, he seems to derive much satisfaction from helping his fellow 'students'—an activity I believe is called 'tutoring.'"

"'Tutoring,' eh? The charity these creatures show toward each other disgusts me. Does he have any other notable characteristics?"

"Yes. The one that interested me the most is what they call a good 'sense of humor,' something quite unknown on our planet since ancient times. It seems that the ability to percieve things in a 'humorous' way and make other creatures 'laugh' is highly prized on the Earth. This ability enables one to make friends and generally put other Earthlings at ease."

"This . . . 'sense of humor,' did you say? seems a most illogical trait. We Nerfonians have advanced quite highly without such a thing. I suppose I should not let it bother me; there are many things about these Earthlings which defy understanding. Besides, you are the cultural expert; if you think we can gain a foothold in 'Brown University' through this 'Eric Maki,' we might as well try it. When shall we instruct the technicains back on Nerfon to begin the contrustion of an android to replace him?"

"I think it would be wise, Zilbub, to return home and wait awhile. The only possible hitch in my plan would be a 'rejection letter,' a notice to Eric Maki that he has been denied admission."

"And what if he is rejected, Zarkon, what then?"

"Obviously, my dear Zilbub, the next step would be to replace the Brown admissions staff with our androids. We would then be able to admit anyone we wanted. Think of it—we could admit a student body made up entirely of Nerfonian spy clones—what a glorious day that would be! But for the moment, we must be patient; the admissions decision will not be final for several Earth 'months.'"

"I am curious, Zarkon, as to what will become of the original Eric Maki after our android has replaced him?"

"I was contemplating depositing him in the interplanetary zoo on Nerfon. He has several other talents which might be interesting to visitors there. Spends much time attached to a thing called a 'saxophone,' creating weird and chilling sounds. He also rides a device called a 'bicycle' great distances at high velocities for no apparent reason. An exhibit like that could cause a larger sensation than the four-headed grooble from Dorcon IV. We could be two extremely rich Nerfonians for capturing such a one."

"You are shrewder than I had previously thought, Zarkon. But as you say, we must wait until the 'month' of 'April.' Let us set a course for home."

"Yes, Zilbub. I long to breathe the sweet, fresh methane of our atmosphere again."

Their conversation ended, the two aliens move their craft out of orbit and back out into the inky blackness of space . . .

COMMENT:

Thumbs up for the high degree of creativity displayed here. This will surely grab and hold the attention of the earth creatures on the admissions committee. Eric is a talented writer, with a fine sense of humor, and many other positive things to offer his college. The downside is that most of the information about himself contained in the essay represents information found elsewhere—already—in Eric's application materials. We must applaud this original approach to answering the question—but should also caution against gimmickry for its own sake. There are a few spelling errors Eric should have spotted: "access," "perceive," "technician." (RJO)

William Meyerhofer
College: Harvard University

THE TRIAL

(As the lights slowly rise, a spot distinguishes the suspect alone in the middle of the stage. He is sitting in a rigid, uncomfortable-looking wooden chair. His ankle is handcuffed to a chair leg. High above him, behind a glass booth, such as is the kind used in recording studios, sit three shadowy figures, the judges. There is a great deal of clicking and scratching of the sort made by microphones when they are first turned on. Finally, there is a long, piercing cry of feedback, and a blowing on an overamplified microphone. Judge 1 has the voice of a bored clerk.)

Judge 1: Your name please?

The Suspect: What?

J1: Your name, please?

Suspect: Will Meyerhofer.

J1: Do you know why you're here?

S: Here?

J1: Being judged.

Judge 2: He's playing stupid.

Judge 3: Shhh!

J1: You have been accused of uselessness. How do you plead?

S: Plead?

J2: Really . . .

J3: Shhh!

J1: Please answer the following question in any way you can. Tell us about an extracurricular activity which is important to you and which you think will help us know you better.

S: Well, I write. And I . . .

J2: We've read your writing, Meyerhofer. It's pretty pitiful.

J3: *(A female voice, rather condescending)* Oh, yes, all the adjectives! Cliches galore . . .

J2: Shhh!

J1: Can you think of anything else?

S: *(thinking)* I play the bass . . .

J1: Anything useful?

S: Perhaps less than I'd thought.

J2: Suspect pleads guilty.

J1: We are going to run quickly over a list of your more glaring faults, Mr. Meyerhofer. Please stop us if anything should strike your particular interest. You talk too much. You don't know how to punctuate conversation. You like to sit with your sneakers on the wallpaper. You often forget to walk your dog. You never clean your contact lenses. You curse. You are arrogant, . . . let's see . . . you don't practice the piano . . .

S: Is this really necessary?

J3: We're only doing this for your own good.

S: Just tell me why I'm supposed to be useless.

J2: It's simple, you don't accomplish anything of use to the rest of the world.

J1: You wander around in a haze, Meyerhofer, paying no attention to anyone around you. What's your greatest ambition?

S: To go to Harvard.

J2: You're as good as lost, kid.

J3: Why don't you take up something useful? Like soccer, or student government?

J3: Or speaking Arabic, or Hindi?

J1: Or a varsity letter, or a piano competition.

J3: Make something of yourself. Perfect your character.

J2: Yes, make yourself perfect.

S: But no one is perfect. You couldn't find someone who does everything well.

J2: Of course we could.

J3: We do it all the time.

J1: Do you honestly think that everyone is as useless as yourself?

S: Well, I do believe that no one is perfect.

J2: If you insist, then we'll prove it to you. Call in the last witness.

J1: He's fairly average, but he'll do.

(There is a short pause, then the witness walks onto the stage. He is every senior's nightmare, the perfect kid. He is immaculately dressed, down to the penny loafers and a wool tie. He sits comfortably beneath the judges.)

J3: *(In a sickeningly sweet voice)* Good afternoon.

Witness: Hello, and how are you today?

J2: We're just fine. Anything we can get you?

W: No thank you, I'm fine, beautiful day.

J2: Yes, it is lovely.

J1: We called you here to tell us a little something about yourself.

W: Well, I'm terribly modest, but I'm at the top of my class in every subject.

J2: That's just wonderful.

W: I play varsity hockey, tennis, lacrosse, wrestling, cross-country, squash, handball, backgammon, and chess.

J3: That's good to hear.

W: I read Sanskrit fluently, and dance, and star in every school play, and have bicycled across the country, and won the Tchaikovsky piano competition.

J1: Thank you, that's just grand. We'll see you later.

J2: Yes, bye-bye.

J3: Take care.

(The witness leaves. There is a silence.)

S: So that's the competition.

J1: What?

S: I'm a little discouraged, that's all.

J1: Cheer up, we'll make something of you yet. Here's the next question: What's your Social Security number?

S: I don't know. What is it?

J1: This is no time for games, Mr. Meyerhofer.

S: How could my Social Security number possibly have any relevance to this hearing? I object.

J2: Objection denied on the grounds that it may be a good Social Security number or a bad Social Security number. Read the school philosophy concerning such matters to the suspect, if you would.

J3: Ahem. In its effort to maintain a fair and comprehensive admissions policy, the court has found it appropriate to give equal consideration to both the applicant's classroom grades and the numbers, such as SAT scores, ACT scores, school CEEB numbers, Social Security numbers, birthdates, expected dates of graduation from the aforesaid institution, and dates of graduation of the parent or guardian of the accused, which have been assigned and considered appropriate by the institution of assignation. Is that quite clear?

S: Yes, I think so.

J2: You see, Mr. Meyerhofer, these numbers are the only standardized basis on which we can base our considerations. I don't like numbers either, when I dial '0' on the telephone, I like to talk to a person, not a machine.

J3: Hear, hear.

J2: But these numbers simply must be considered.

J1: Very well put.

J3: Yes, perfectly concise and comprehendable.

J1: Now, what is the birthdate of your maternal grandmother? Please give us the best date possible. We will discard the lowest date.

S: May 1, 1908.

J2: Thank you. Next question. Please describe how you expect to change during your four years in college.
   (Silence)

J1: Well?

S: I don't know. I've never gone to college before.

J3: But surely you must know what you're in for.

J2: You must have seen what other people are like when they get out of college?

S: They just seem older, I guess. And they know more.

J2: This is ridiculous. Call in the other witness!

J1: I've never heard of such a thing. What is he going to college for, anyway? Employment?

(The perfect kid reenters, with a Walkman around his head.)

W: *(In a bored monotone)* I expect my four years in college to be years of profound personal and intellectual growth, a time when I will have the freedom and resources at my disposal to expand and broaden the scope of my vision of mankind.

J1: Oh, now that was lovely.

S: But what exactly did it all mean? What "scope of vision"?

J3: Please!

J2: If you cannot appreciate another's true superiority, you might as well be quiet.

J1: *(To the witness)* That was very nice. Do say hello to your father for me. He was a Yale man, wasn't he?

W: What?

J1: Well, I'm pretty sure of it. Bye now.

(Witness leaves.)

J2: Now, are you going to be helpful, or do we have to sit here all day?

S: *(Bitterly)* I will expand my horizons.

J3: Very good. Next:

J2: Tell us about a book which has changed you, which you have read in the last six weeks, and which was not a required-reading book. It must be between one hundred and fifty and four hundred pages, written between 1830 and 1952, and well known to our admissions staff.

J3: May we suggest *The Catcher in the Rye.*

J2: Or Shakespeare's *Faust.*

J3: Or *Spanish Lace,* by Joyce Dingwell.

S: Well, I remember *Remembrance of Things Past,* by Proust.

J1: Too long.

S: I read *The Magic Mountain,* by Thomas Mann.

J3: Never heard of it.

S: I read *Crime and Punishment*.

J2: What's that?

S: *Crime and Punishment*.

J1: Isn't that that Russian thing?

J3: I know I've heard of it.

J2: Probably just obscure. Book accepted. Now then, Mr. Meyerhofer, are you applying for very early admission, fairly early admission, earlier than most admission, regular admission, late admission, blueberry admission, guava admission, rectilinear admission, rolling admissions, bouncing admissions, or large green admissions with fur on their teeth?

S: The former, I think.

J2: Excellent choice. You must have your application in by yesterday afternoon.

S: That doesn't give me much time.

J1: We're just trying to treat you like an adult, Mr. Meyerhofer.

J3: The real world isn't a bed of roses, I can tell you that.

S: I'll do my best.

J2: Now for the part of the application process which we are personally very proud of, the personal statement.

J1: Yes, this is the brand-new part of the process which lends us the important final insights into your character which are so vital to a cooperative and successful admissions experience.

(During the end of the play, perfect students, like the witness, appropriately dressed, are lining up behind the suspect, their dark forms visible, like Macbeth's line of kings.)

J3: We are very proud of the courage it took to grant our applicants this portion of the application to be creative, personal, and irrelevant.

J2: Mr. Meyerhofer, describe for us, in as many words as you wish, in as personal a way as is possible, the relevance of new-triassic polymers in the reproductive cycle of plasmids.

S: The what!?

J1: I told you that it wouldn't work.

J3: Blasted liberals, what more could we do for these brats. Ungrateful termites!

S: What am I supposed to do with a topic like that?

J1: I think it's perfectly clear.

J2: Write, pig!!!

J1: We couldn't have made it clearer.

J3: Do you think we enjoy our jobs? Do you think we enjoy reading your stupid essays? I drink ten cups of coffee a day just to get through this boring job, and I need a bottle of Valium to get to sleep at night.

J1: You don't have to sit and study adolescents all day for a living. You don't have to read this junk all day. You have to understand her feelings.

J2: He'll never understand what he's done, that his generation is singlehandedly destroying all that mankind has worked so hard for. Just go away, you vicious child.

S: But I'm handcuffed to this chair, I can't go away.

(The line of perfect students marches slowly toward him, their arms outstretched, ready to kill.)

Total silence.

(The lights in the glass booth go out, and the suspect stands alone in a slowly shrinking spotlight. He turns to the audience with a look of complete despair, and the spot blacks out.)

Curtain

COMMENT:

What is impressive about the essay is not the theme, which is rather pedestrian, but the form. The writer is clearly and admirably in control of his medium. (TH)

Arun Ramanathan
College: Haverford College

Mental Block is a nasty old hermit who lives in the gullies and ravines of my mind. He makes a living by slinging nets across my neural canals and catches my thoughts as they swim toward the great spawning grounds where writing is born. M.B. always waits until his nets are full to the point of bursting before he drags them up. Like any experienced fisherman, he saves only the big, healthy, mature thoughts and throws juvenile or diseased thoughts back into the canals to mature or die. Those thoughts he saves, he either eats immediately or freezes and sets aside for use when my stream of creativity slows.

Up until three weeks ago, I had always ignored M.B.; his paltry catch consisted of only a small fraction of my thoughts. Lately, however, with college essays to write, M.B. has become an increasingly irritating problem. Many of my best thoughts begin their journey through my mind only to be poached and eaten before they can breed and create others like them.

So, with college deadlines looming, I set off in search of the old hermit, determined to somehow halt his activities, if only temporarily. Finding him was no problem. The recent flood of thoughts accompanying my latest attempts at creativity had so fattened him that he was uninclined to move about. Instead, he sat in the center of my mind at the junction of a number of important canals, wielding his net with practiced expertise. M.B. pulled in one load after another, emptying them from his nets in a flopping, jumbled tangle.

He frowned when he saw me approaching and shifted to face me, his motion scattering the skeletons of countless thoughts. I picked my way toward him, through heaps of such skeletons, stopping at the base of a particularly large one upon which M.B. was seated. "What cha want?" he snapped, peering down at me over his massive, bloated waistline. Before I could reply, he angrily muttered, "C'mon ya gotta want somethin'; you ain't one ta come visitin' fer no reason."

"I want to make a deal," I replied.

"A deal, with me, how nice of ya, now what kinda deal were ya thinkin' of makin', my boy?" he said, his lips curling into a sneer.

"I want you to stop stealing my thoughts until after college deadlines . . ."

"And if I should do this?" he interjected.

"I'll do whatever you want."

"Well, my boy, let me tell you." He paused, shifting into a more comfortable posture. "I'll make this deal with ya if ye'll do me two things."

"What two things?" I asked, dreading his answer.

M.B. picked up a bone and began to wave it at me in school-teacher fashion. "You know, my boy, I've been doin' this job fer sometime now, seventeen years at last count, and over this time yer thoughts have been getting' progressively better. Over these last four years, boy, not only has the fishin' improved, but yer thoughts have been bigger, healthier, and more mature."

"So what are the two things?" I questioned, irritated.

He ignored me. "Especially when ya tried ta write poetry last year, my, that was some good fishin'; and that term paper, 'Richard III and The Prince: the Villain and the Pragmatist,' whooo whee, that was some good eatin'."

"No wonder I could never write poetry or organize that stupid paper," I muttered under my breath.

"Well, gettin' back to my point, I'll stop my fishin'—fer the time bein'—if ye'll apply to Haverford and take liberal arts if ya get in."

"What??!!"

"See boy, the thing is; if ya get into Haverford, I figure ye'll have so many term papers and stuff ta write that I'll be feastin' regular fer more'n four years."

"But what about the liberal arts?"

"Well, boy, in my many years at this fishin', I've caught yer liberal arts thoughts and I've caught yer science and math thoughts, and, when ya get right down to it, yer liberal arts thoughts are just much tastier. They're so much more natural and healthy. Them science and math thoughts just taste so processed and mechanical. It's like the difference between filet mignon and Spam; see?"

"Yeh, I do," I replied. "You got a deal."

M.B. held out his great, pudgy hand, which I grabbed and shook. "Ye'll know when I'm back in business," he said, giving me a wink.

"And by the way," he shouted, as I walked away. "You better get into Haverford; I ain't starvin' fer nothin'."

Karen Steinig
College: Brown University

Through the wee hours of the morning, during the time between *Late Night with David Letterman* and reruns of *Ben Casey,* I stayed awake, sitting on the carpet and gnawing my pencil. Sane people were sleeping. Yet here I was alone in my room with the television droning in the background, agonizing over "this opportunity to tell us about anything you think we should know." After yet another sales pitch for imported bamboo steamers (just $19.95), something on the TV screen caught my eye. Lights flashed, bells rang, and then . . .

"Hey there, ladies and gentlemen, and welcome to . . . THE AD-MISSIONS GAME! You all know the rules: There are none! Our players will be competing for a chance at the Grand Prize: a four-year trip to . . . Providence, Rhode Island!"

"Ooooooh . . ." sighed the studio audience. "Aaaaah . . ."

The host continued. "Here are today's players. Why don't you introduce yourselves, kids?"

The three teenagers glanced about nervously. "Ah'm Becky Sue Smith," drawled Player #1.

"I'm Joe Jock," mumbled Player #2.

"And I'm Karen Steinig," said Player #3.

The host went on. "We've got a great mix of opponents here. Let's get under way. First question. Be careful, it's a tricky one: Where do you live?" Player #1 slammed the buzzer. "Yes, Becky Sue?"

"Ah'm from Vandervoort, Arkansas," squealed Player #1 with a knowing grin.

"Good answer! Good answer!" cried the audience.

"All right!" shouted the host. "Ten points to Player #1 for Geographical Diversity! Don't feel bad about not getting to the button first, Karen; Long Island is the wrong answer anyway. Next question: How do you spend your free time?"

This time Player #2 was the first to the buzzer. "I play football," he rumbled. The alumni in the audience stood up, cheered, and threw $20 bills like confetti.

"Excellent!" exclaimed the host. "Ten Endowment Points for Joe Jock! Don't feel bad about not getting to the button first, Karen; badminton is the wrong answer anyway. Well, things are really sizzling here, but Karen seems to be at a bit of a disadvantage. Let's see how she does with question number three. Everyone ready? Okay. Why do you want to attend Brown University? Yes! Player #1, Becky Sue Smith."

"Ah'd like to take all thirty-two courses S/NC." BZZZZ!

"Spare me," groaned the host. "Let's hope for a little more depth from Player #2, Joe Jock."

"Uh, well," he stumbled, sweating beneath his shoulder pads, "I hear those Ivy League women are pretty hot." BZZZZ!

"Not quite what we were looking for. How about you, Karen?" Player #3 cleared her throat and stood up straight. She knew her answer to this one. "I want to be part of Brown University," she began, "because I'm more motivated, more disciplined, when I have the freedom to choose not to be. You see, I am—"

"Thank you, Karen," said the host. "That's just fine. And now, a few words from our—"

"Excuse me, but I'm not finished. As I was saying, I am my own harshest critic; therefore, my biggest challenges are the ones that I alone seek to create, not the ones that are imposed upon me by outside sources. Paradoxically, I'd be roused to take a wide variety of courses at Brown because there are no distribution requirements. Brown would trust me to make responsible choices about my education, and when I'm treated as an adult, I become one."

The crowd roared, whistles blew, balloons fell from the sky. "Well, folks," yelled the host, "it seems as if only Karen Steinig will move on to the big bonus round and try for that Grand Prize . . . four years in Providence (a metaphor if ever I heard one). But we won't let our losers go away empty-handed. For Becky Sue and Joe Jock, a very nice consolation prize . . . six months' training at Wilfred Beauty Academy! And we'll be right back after these messages."

During the commercial break I went down to the kitchen for a fourth cup of coffee, cursing myself for vegetating in front of a TV game show when I should have been working on my application. November 15 was quickly approaching, and I still had no essay. My little sister's advice made it seem so easy: "Just write something that tells them you're smart, creative, spirited, artistic, and funny." Sure, but how? Frustrated and bleary-eyed, I trudged upstairs.

When I entered my room, I was greeted by the final strains of the national anthem. Apparently I missed the final bonus rounds of that game, so I don't know how it all turned out. To tell you the truth, I'm sort of curious. If you happen to have been up late that night and you saw some unusual programming coming across the airwaves, tell me what went on. Did Player #3 win the Grand Prize trip to Providence, or did she wind up with the dining room furniture and a year's supply of Turtle Wax? Let me know around mid-December, okay? Thanks.

COMMENT:

Nice. Tight, introductory paragraph that sets the mood but doesn't belabor it. The game show section is creatively done, not too involved, and filled with appropriate and funny phrases that have been borrowed from real game shows. The game show format ties into the admissions process, but the writer does not force the connection too far. On the other hand, the writer is clearly writing the essay for Brown, and s/he cleverly, using Karen (contestant #3), presents her rather full understanding of Brown's academic program and the kind of student who will benefit most from it, despite the potentially awkward context. This writer has an excellent ear for dialogue and a very mature sense of what will succeed in being humorous. (AST)

Kristin Ward
College: Dartmouth College

I would like to explain to you how it all happened. The day I took my SATs started out as a perfectly normal January day in New Hampshire. I woke up with icicles hanging off my ears. I swung my feet onto my bedroom floor, which was as warm as a polar ice cap, and then I slunk down to breakfast, harboring the bitter realization that every step I took brought me farther away from the comfort of my pillow and quilt.

As I sat at the kitchen table, I wished that I could discreetly dive into my mug of hot chocolate to combat the frostbite which I had contracted on the way downstairs.

Merely a red blur of scarf, hat, and mittens against the thick white snow, I trudged down the driveway to my car.

I was halfway to Concord, the testing site, when, all of a sudden, I came upon the mind-boggling scene. I coaxed my eyes back into their sockets and hit the brakes. Less than ten feet away from my Volkswagen, there were three aqua creatures, shaped like gigantic mushrooms with arms and legs. They were seated in the middle of the road and they seemed to be meditating.

My wits were still scattered all over the car when one of the three creatures, having noticed my presence, came over to address me.

The creature raised his arm in what seemed to be a harmless greeting, and began to speak: "I am Sug. I am on a mission from a distant star. One of the masters of our species has died . . ."

"My condolences," I interrupted weakly.

"Thank you," the creature continued. "We have decided to start a new tradition in our culture. We observed it on your planet. I am referring to the custom of engraved tombstones. My associates (he paused and gestured to the two meditating mushrooms) and I stopped at a gas station and we were told to come to New Hampshire, 'the Granite State,' to get a slab for our master's tombstone. So here we are. Can you please assist us?"

Several maxims surfaced in my mind: Don't talk to strangers (especially ones who resemble mushrooms); be hospitable to guests (especially foreigners); be on time for tests (especially SATs).

I glanced at my watch nervously. If I did not get to the test center in ten minutes, I would be late. The creature was leaning on my car, waiting for an answer.

"I'm very sorry," I said. "I would like to help you, but I am taking my SATs today and I can't be late."

The creature looked puzzled. "SATs?" he asked, tilting his head inquisitively.

"They're hard to explain," I said, "and I really must be going."

Sug scratched his head thoughtfully. "No, I'm sorry," he said. "You will have to help us *now*. We must get back to our people soon. They are anxiously awaiting our return. As soon as you have helped us, you can go to your SATs."

I considered my alternatives: I could try to make a break for it and be pummeled by three extraterrestrial beings in search of a tombstone, or I could help them with their mission and then pray that I would be admitted to the testing center a little late.

I noticed that Sug's two associates were now up and walking toward my car, so I quickly decided to go with the latter option.

"I'm not sure, right offhand, where we can get a slab of granite," I said. "I'll have to go back to my house to get a phone book. I am sure there will be a listing in the Yellow Pages."

It was fortunate that the creatures had some invisible flying mechanism, because it was quite obvious that they would not fit into my car. Constantly glancing at my watch, I drove back to my house. To spare my family the shock I had experienced, I politely asked the creatures to wait outside while I consulted the Yellow Pages.

"All right, I've found a place," I said, feigning enthusiasm. "It's about twenty minutes from here."

They flew alongside the car as I drove to the quarry. (You can imagine the stares!)

The man at the quarry was very helpful—even if he was in shock. The creatures were very satisfied with the tombstone, which they had engraved on the premises, and then tied onto Sug's back for the journey home. Before leaving, he thanked me profusely.

"Thank you so much," Sug said. "Our people will be forever grateful. And good luck on your SATs."

My face turned white as a sheet. I had forgotten all about them. I looked at my watch. The tests would be almost over by now.

I arrived at the testing center in an absolute panic. I tried to tell my story, but my sentences and descriptive gestures got so confused that I communicated nothing more than a very convincing version of a human tornado. In an effort to curb my distracting explanation, the proctor led me to an empty seat and put a test booklet in front of me. He looked doubtfully from me to the clock, and then he walked away.

I tried desperately to make up for lost time, scrambling madly through analogies and sentence completions.

"Fifteen minutes remain," the voice of doom declared from the front of the classroom.

Algebraic equations, arithmetic calculations, geometric diagrams swam before my eyes.

"Time! Pencils down, please."

"Thanks a lot, Sug," I thought, when I saw my math score six weeks later.

Naturally, I attributed the disastrous 480 to him. He had been in a difficult situation, of course, with his people depending on him and all, so I decided, in my mind, to forgive him. I felt a little less gracious, however, when I was halfway to the SAT testing center in June, and there he was *again,* an oversized blue mushroom in the middle of the road . . .

ESSAYS ON COMING TO AMERICA

Anonymous
College: Princeton University

I think I began to grow up that winter night when my parents and I were returning from my aunt's house, and my mother said that we might soon be leaving Leningrad to go to America. We were in the Metro then. I was crying, and some people in the car were turning around to look at me. I remember that I could not bear the thought of never hearing again the radio program for schoolchildren to which I listened every morning before going to school.

I do not remember myself crying for this reason again. In fact, I think I cried very little when I was saying goodbye to my friends, relatives, and even to my father. When we were leaving I thought about all the places I was going to see—the strange and magical countries I had known only from adventure books and pictures in the world atlas; I even learned the names of the fifty states because their sound was so beautifully foreign and mysterious. The country I was leaving never to come back was hardly in my head then.

The four years that followed taught me the importance of optimism, but the notion did not come at once. For the first two years in New York I was really lost—coming from a school in Leningrad to a Brooklyn yeshiva, and then to Chapin, I did not quite know what I was or what I should be. Mother remarried, and things became even more complicated for me. Some time passed before my stepfather and I got used to each other. I was often upset, and saw no end to "the hard times."

My responsibilities in the family increased dramatically since I knew English better than everyone else at home. I wrote letters, filled out forms, translated at interviews with Immigration and Social Security officers, took my grandparents to the doctor and translated there, and even discussed telephone and utilities bills with company representatives. I spent a lot of time at my grandparents' house, and eventually moved in with them.

As a result of my experiences I have learned one very important rule: Ninety-nine percent of all common troubles eventually go away! Something good is bound to happen in the end when you do not give up, and just wait a little! Of course, troubles need help in getting out of our lives, but I do not mind putting in a little work. For some reason I believe that my life will turn out all right, even though it will not be very easy.

America gave us freedom and independence. It also made us assume the responsibility for ourselves. Nobody can ruin my life unless I let it be ruined. We create our own happiness. It is up to us to use our freedom with responsibility.

When I was twelve I read a book about a girl growing up in tzarist Russia. Her grandfather once told her, "Life is like a zebra. There are white and black stripes on it. When you are on a white stripe walk slowly, enjoy it. When you come to a black stripe raise your collar, shut your eyes, and run as fast as you can go to get to a white one. But remember, there is always a white stripe after a black one!"

COMMENT:

The opening is very powerful because it grabs the reader and creates suspense. She also talks about difficulties without any self-pity or a self-congratulatory attitude. The anecdote at the end is very good too; it ties the essay together. (PT)

Sayantan Deb
College: Harvard University

I looked at my mother, awestruck. What she had just said played back in my mind. Looking out of the window, she had smiled. "You know, the locals call them *Babla.*" My name, my house-name, the name she had always called me by was *Babla*. I had never really asked her where my name came from. It was just something I had taken for granted. That morning, when my mother and I had stood in the middle of a crowded Howrah station, I had no idea that I would find out.

The train was late. The summer sun glared angrily at us. It was one of those days when the humidity from the Ganges became a tangible presence. You could feel the claustrophobic blanket around you, but you couldn't take it off. The train crawled in taking its sweet time and a swarm of people flooded the station. My mom grabbed my hand and pushed through the crowd. I was lost in the throng of people, so I let my mom's hand guide me into the compartment.

We were going to my mother's university hospital. As the train pulled out of the station, the scene around me changed rapidly. The tracks by the Ganges quickly said goodbye to the distant cityscape, and gave way to large tracts of farmland. The land was shining in different shades of green, punctuated by an occasional house. My mother was eagerly looking outside. She hadn't been here in seventeen years.

As the farmlands turned into a town outside our windows, the train began to slow down, and pulled into a small station. We took an auto-rickshaw for the next stretch of the trip. Soon, we entered a tree-lined stretch of road. The trees bent over from both sides, giving the appearance of arches. I looked outside, fascinated. They weren't very good looking, neither tall, nor regal. In fact, they were quite flimsy. My mother asked me what I was looking at. I pointed out to her the trees that made those gateways. She smiled. "You know, the locals call them *Babla.*"

My mother told me that when she was pregnant she would go through this tree-lined stretch of road every day. It was her favorite part of the five-hour journey. The trees were very resilient. Unlike in Kolkata, the climate here was prone to severe droughts. Even in challenging conditions, they would live, embrace their climate, and they would survive.

I discovered in that trip that just like the trees, I had been brought up to be resilient. I had been taught to never give up in the face of adversity, but to face it head on, and give my best. I was plucked away from my familiar Kolkata, my friends, and the house that I grew up in. I could have wilted in a new country, in classrooms where for months I would not understand the language or the people. There were times when I would cry to my mom, tell her that I wanted to leave. She told me to hang on. So, I spent recesses trying to talk to people, ignoring their snide remarks. I wanted to absorb my environment, assimilate into the culture as best I could. Now, I have made a new home. I have grown to enjoy the once unfamiliar snowy winters, rainy springs, and golden wind-swept falls. I have thrived, amongst a new set of friends, and a new school. The red maple leaves that blanket my lawn every October have become my *Krishnachura,* the crimson flowers that swept over my house in Kolkata every autumn.

On our ride back to the city, my mother told me that if she had wanted to, she could have taken a job in Kolkata. Instead, she had spent the first three years of her career in rural India, undertaking a five-hour journey every day to the understaffed hospital. She believed that the people in the area had needed her help. She felt indebted to the hospital where she had been trained, where she had held a scalpel for the first time, the place where she had felt the cold steely familiarity of a stethoscope around her neck for the first time. So, she had decided to stay on as a doctor in that hospital. She told me that it was important to stay grounded in the places where we came from. That is what still brings me back to Kolkata almost every year, for nine years. After all, Kolkata embraced me in my first winters, told me that I would be fine. Its feeling of acceptance was what I used to hang on to in those lonely recesses. Although I have a new home, my roots still reach a city that is seven seas away.

The trip with my mother had been more than a glimpse of a distant past. It had been a journey to a place which was familiar to me even before I was born, a place which had played hide-and-seek with me for seventeen years, peeking into every aspect of my present. In fact, this trip had been a journey to something very fundamental—my name, my character, my identity.

COMMENT:

The theme in this essay is well presented, making a clear connection to the applicant's nickname, weaving his heritage, culture and family values. The writer achieves this without being overbearing or pretentious. He uses descriptive words that "fit" and are well placed. The writer also paints a picture, employing all the senses, and the reader is easily transported to the crowded street and the farmland. As for critique, the writer's time line could be confusing. He begins with a moment of awe, then moves back to how he arrived at that moment, then moves forward. It reads slightly askew; however the point is still there for a take away. (BLB)

Thai Pham
College: Brown University

Uproot a tree and replant it. Chances are very high that the tree will have difficulty surviving. If you do the equivalent to a human, the poor person will have the same problem. Yet he could usually overcome it. Though this may have some physiological implications, it is also a matter of will. A person fights both physically and mentally. He never gives up, because by doing so he renounces all chances of a victory. In my case, leaving Vietnam and coming to the U.S. is the equivalence of being uprooted and replanted someplace else. In the course of this painful change, I learned that the secret to successfully achieving a goal is tenacity.

At the beginning of my journey, I observed and admired the tenacious quality in my parents. All I could remember in the early stages of our escape is that occasionally I was taken out of the city, only to return the next day. Later, I learned that those were the unsuccessful attempts to escape from communism. Eleven times my family tried; eleven times we were swindled. Eleven times we risked imprisonment, yet eleven times we were lucky. Our family resources were being exhausted at an astonishing rate. Family heirlooms were exchanged for the hope of freedom. The next time could have been the last, but we did not quit. We invested everything in the twelfth attempt. Looking back, I realize that it would have been so easy to quit during any step of the way. Repeated failures could have discouraged us, but we kept on trying. Finally, we were lucky. The people were honest. We thought that we had succeeded.

However, a great ocean still separated us from freedom. Storms with towering waves tossed our small boat about indifferently. A well-equipped vessel would have had problems dealing with such a storm; but we had only a high school world map and Boy Scout compass as navigation tools. Later, even these were taken by pirates. Our food and water supplies became practically nonexistent in the last few days of our journey. Getting lost at sea did not do much for morale. Nevertheless, we held onto our goal though it would have been easier to resign our fate to the currents. With determination, we conquered the elements, and arrived safely at the refugee camp.

When we reached the U.S., new problems surfaced. I had dealt with thirst and hunger on the boat, but humiliation requires an extra something. I entered the third grade with practically no understanding of the English language. At school, I was not well received. The other students looked down at me because of my inability to speak English well. I can still remember the times in spelling class when the teacher went down the list: "Who has one wrong? . . . Two wrong? . . . Thirty wrong . . ." I would always be the last to raise my hand, and the only one to receive zeros on these assignments. Instead of giving up, I became more determined to conquer my problems, both in and out of the classroom.

By the second semester, my hard work was paying off. On the playground, I was making new friends. In the classroom, I was making new friends. The door was finally opened for me, but it took a lot of effort. There were times that I wanted to stay home, times that I did not want to face another day of humiliation, and times that I wished we were back in Vietnam. But I remembered my parents' example: They did not quit when the situation seemed hopeless. My journey to the U.S. has taught me a valuable lesson: "Winners never quit, and quitters never win." I have applied this lesson to solve my problems in adapting to a new environment, and I expect this attitude to help me overcome those problems I may encounter in the future.

COMMENT:

The impact of this essay comes more from the reader's realization of what the writer has experienced than from the "telling of the tale" or the writing. No matter, the impact is a very strong one, and the opening analogy, comparing the uprooting of a person with the uprooting of a tree, is a very powerful image, which sticks with the reader throughout. The rest of the essay conveys, in a poignant way, just how significant a part the values of family, determination, hope, and courage have *already* played in the life of this young person. One can only imagine what a wonderful adult s/he will become. (AST)

Nzuekoh Nvepowoh Nchinda
College: Yale University

CAMEROON

I stood at the edge, watching the river rush by. My stomach tightened with remembrance of the fear that had gripped me the first day I stood at this spot, reluctant to step foot on the plank bridge. I remember clutching onto my mother's hand and placing one hesitant foot before the other, eyeing the violent waters below my feet. Now, the same bridge lay before me, but this time I had no hand to hold onto. This time, I did not need one.

Four years of separation had strengthened the bond I felt to this land. So deeply submerged in a profound sense of familiarity, I let the memories wash over me. My mind flooded, I felt a rushing calm that buried the seedlings of apprehension and pushed me forward. Finally, my feet sank into the deep mud of the opposite side. I watched the thick, brown liquid ooze between my toes. I committed the soft texture to my memories. I looked over the green stalks before me, catching a glimpse of the top of the familiar burgundy roof. Eyes set on it, I ran through the field. Once I was through the field, my feet continued to pound upon the extensive dirt road, until I reached the gate.

The white block with its burgundy cap was stately seated upon the dirt floors. This is where I spoke and wrote my first English words. Back then, I never imagined that I would be living in a world where English was not confined within school walls. I ran my fingers along the rusting gates, memorizing the contours of the intricately twisted metal. I let the white walls fill my vision. When I closed my eyes, I heard the shouts of the older children as they ran toward the gate. I heard the cries of my fellow new young ones who clutched their sisters and mothers. I heard my mother say to me, "Nah-Nah, go." The first day still felt like yesterday.

I turned from the gate and ran back through the fields. I ran across the bridge. I ran back into the bustling streets and sounds of town. I passed the children and their makeshift game of tires, the lady selling 'egusi' and fried plantains and the deep laughter of men chatting over bottles of Guinness. I stopped in front of my grandmother's blue block of a home, recognizing the aroma of wholesome country 'jama jama' permeating the arid air of the dry season. My grandmother called, "Nah-Nah, it is time to eat."

I stood a moment longer, committing the aridness, the aroma, and the timbre of my grandmother's voice to memory. I had to commit it all to memory for I didn't know when I would have this opportunity again. I had to remember. This was my home. I knew that in a week I would no longer wake up to the African sun.

COMMENT:

This is an incredibly strong admissions essay. It is both well-written and powerful. In this essay, she combines cultural flavor with personal growth. This essay begins with the writer describing the ritual of boarding a boat to leave Cameroon. She suggests that this is something that has happened multiple times and how at first, being scared, she required her mother to make her feel safe. Four years since leaving Cameroon, she returns with a renewed connection to the land and the people in it, but knowing that she must leave again soon she faces the bittersweet task of saying goodbye to her homeland once more. Skillfully, she brings the reader on her journey as she races through the streets visiting once-familiar places. This essay has a beautiful sense of time, shown most clearly at the end of the essay when she writes the paragraph that begins "I stood a moment longer . . ." The reason why this essay is so successful is that in discussing the passage of time and her departures from her homeland she shows how much she has grown through the years and how she is preparing for the next phase of her life, which presumably is college. (AMH)

Baffour Osei
College: Duke University

BRIDGES

When I lived in Ghana, I would ride my bike home every day after school . . . but little did I know that it would almost cost me my life.

Soaking in sweat from the sub-Saharan heat, I came to a fork in the road. My options were to take a shorter path with a bridge, weakened severely by recent storms, or to take a longer path, which, though significantly more arduous would ensure my safe passage. As a reckless thirteen-year-old boy, I wanted the fast way.

I pedaled out onto the bridge quickly, hoping to fly across, when suddenly the support structure began to give way. Slamming on the breaks, I could feel the metal begin to contort beneath my wheels and was thrown by the jarring motion against the guardrails. The bridge was falling.

I now had a new decision to make: whether to continue forward and hope to make it across or to crawl back the way I had come. Though it would have been safer to crawl back, I pressed forward, pushing my bike up the other side and then climbing up myself.

I feel very blessed that my foolhardiness did not cost me my life, but this story has become significant to me in a number of ways. In a way, it helps to illustrate many of my character traits, namely, my willingness to take risks and the fact that I do not let fear hold me back. Though, yes, this has led me into some interesting predicaments at times, being a risk-taker also gives me the courage I need to try new things and to excel at them. One example of this is how I came from having never played team sports in Ghana to making and remaining on the championship-winning varsity football team in one of the most competitive conferences in the West.

The other main reason why this event is so meaningful to me is that it helps to demonstrate some of the basic challenges of daily life for many Ghanaians. It is almost unthinkable to picture towns and villages dependent on roads that can collapse or become unserviceable without warning. My hope is that with a college education, I can return to Ghana and work to alleviate some of the issues plaguing my country. Collapsing bridges, a lack of running water and unpredictable power outages are not things that many of my peers have experienced, but for me, these things were a fact of life. Though many have grown to accept these problems as commonplace, I believe that they need not be. As of right now I am unsure if I will become an engineer or a humanitarian aid worker, but I know that getting a college education will allow me to explore these ideas and be around bright and creative students, and instructors, who can help me develop a plan for how I can have the most positive impact on my country and hopefully affect lives of millions.

DRAWINGS AND CARTOONS

Paul K. Min
College: Yale University

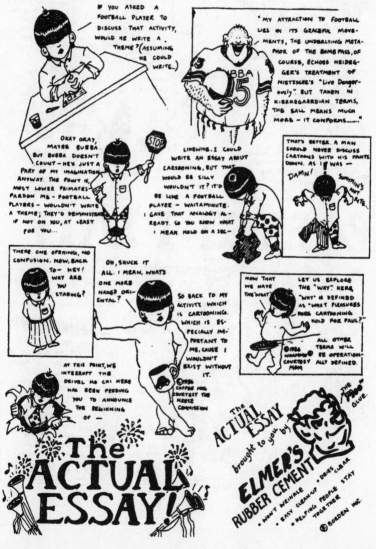

COMMENTS:

A very creative, attention-getting yet risky approach to the essay question. It reveals a witty, imaginative, and daring personality. The cartoon essay appears a bit disjointed at times. The cartoons help to mask the occasional lack of creativity. (TG)

How can the reader not be impressed with Paul's talent, imagination, and willingness to take a risk? So many students feel bound by words and an 8½" x 11" page—not Paul, who clearly reveals his personality through cartoons. (JWM)

Zoe Mulford
College: Harvard University

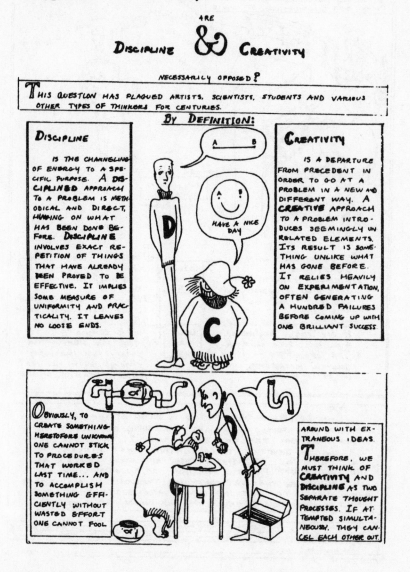

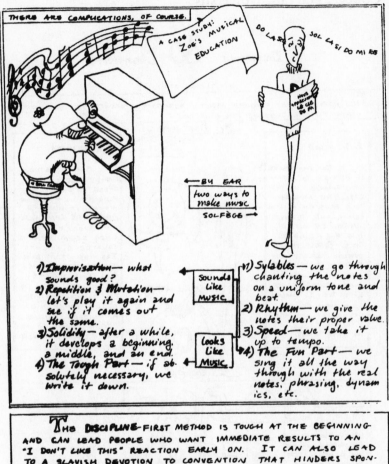

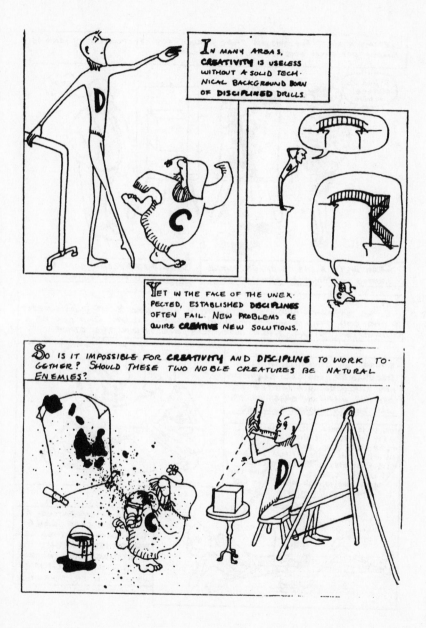

I THINK THE MOST EFFECTIVE PRODUCTS ARE OBTAINED THROUGH FREQUENT — SOMETIMES SPLIT-SECOND — SWITCHES BETWEEN **CREATIVITY** AND **DISCIPLINE**. LONG PROBLEM-SOLVING PRACTICE HELPS ONE TO KNOW WHICH IS NEEDED IN WHAT SITUATIONS. GETTING THIS PRACTICE REQUIRES THE **CREATIVITY** TO EXPERIMENT AND THE **DISCIPLINE** TO STICK AT IT UNTIL IT WORKS...

...AND EVEN THEN THEY CAN BE CAPRICIOUS.

Well, I finally got around to starting this damned Smith thing... but I can't think of anything to write!

What a fantastic idea! ... I suppose I ought to get out of the tub and ... ugh... write it down...

CREATIVITY FAILURE

LACK OF **DISCIPLINE**

AS TO WORKING CREATIVELY ON SCHEDULE, ALL I CAN SAY IS I THOROUGHLY AGREE WITH AGNES DE MILLE. IN AUGUST OF 1986 I LEFT FOR BELGIUM WITH A HALF-WRITTEN COLLEGE ESSAY IN MY SUITCASE. FIVE MONTHS LATER, I'M JUST FINISHING SOMETHING WHICH BEARS VERY LITTLE RESEMBLANCE TO WHAT I STARTED WITH. I GUESS EVERYBODY HAS TO FIND FOR THEMSELVES THEIR PERSONAL **CREATIVITY**/**DISCIPLINE** BALANCE; I'M STILL LOOKING FOR MINE. COLLEGE IS NOT THE ONLY PLACE TO LOOK FOR THIS, BUT IT DOES PRESENT A LOT OF OPPORTUNITIES TO PRACTICE.

WE CAN ALWAYS HOPE.

DC

24/1/87
Zoe Mulford
PATURAGES, BELGIUM

COMMENT:

The real success of this wonderful essay lies in the fact that its very creation is a combination of discipline and creativity. The discipline shows in the substance of the message, the simplicity and clarity of the presentation, and the careful choice of the details and issues presented. The creativity shows in the clever drawings of the figures, whose body shapes, facial expressions, and "thoughts" are so appropriate to the stereotypes the creator is trying to evoke. Ms. Milford not only demonstrates she has a profound understanding of the "apparent" incongruity between discipline and creativity; she demonstrates she also knows how to reconcile the two and use the benefits of each to her great advantage. This essay is a masterful job and a thoroughly enjoyable one to savor. (AST)

Jaeyong So
College: Yale University

COMMENT:

Obvious strengths of the "essay": extraordinary creativity revealed, as well as excellent sense of humor and superior artistic talent (he *does* bring out his real strengths). Drawbacks: This is not an *essay*! We're not sure if he can write at all well. Jaeyung So has placed all his chips in one pile—namely, his artistic gifts. I would question whether or not we as readers have developed any real sense of who this person is, how he thinks, what is important to him, etc. In fact, we should even be a bit concerned if, as the comic strip Jaeyong laments, "I have nothing to write about. I have nothing." How effective this response is would depend on how much about himself (or how little) the writer has included elsewhere in the application. (RJO)

ESSAYS ON DEATH AND DYING

Julie C. Cantor
College: Yale University

Annie was short, white-haired, and about ninety. She had none of the usual signs of age—veined hands, withered appearance, liver-spotted skin. Instead, Annie could have been a friend's grandmother.

Each time I brought her up to therapy, I had to explain to her that Occupational Therapy was the place where she worked on her knitting with Doris. She remembered the knitting, but not Doris, the therapist, or me either. One day when I came to take her to O.T., she said she could not go because her daughter was coming to visit. I told the nursing staff where Annie and I were going so that her daughter could find us. Even so, she asked me five times if her daughter would be able to locate her.

Whenever she saw me she asked if I worked at the home. When I answered no, I was a volunteer, she sweetly replied, "Then you give your time freely. God will bless you and your family." Annie frequently asked if I was still in school. When I told her I was and would be a senior, she said, "How long have you been in school?"

Annie always insisted that she had forgotten how to knit. Yet she knitted beautifully. Puzzled, she would squint and demand that I check to see if she was knitting correctly. She said, "You know, I once dropped a stitch and had to do a whole row over again." I asked her what she wanted to do with the scarf when she had finished. She scrunched up her face and answered, "I don't know. I've made others, but they always take them."

"No, Annie, Doris told me you gave them to your children and grandchildren." I watched as she strained to remember. Annie knew she had lost some of her memory, for she often said, "I'm old and can't remember things the way I used to."

Each time she struggled to see her knitting, until I suggested she wear her glasses. She never knew where they were, even when they hung on a chain around her neck.

When I had to leave her in the middle of a therapy session, she would drop her knitting and beg, "Don't leave me alone. I hate being alone. I need you to help me with my knitting. You won't leave me here, will you? You'll come back?"

Annie frequently wrung her hands in pain, pulling at each joint. Sometimes she dropped her face in her hands. Then she rubbed her watery eyes, lifted her head, knit a few more stitches, and stopped, letting her head fall into her hands again. I wish I could have done something for Annie, but I knew the doctors had already tried everything they could. I hoped her younger years had been happier.

COMMENT:

This is nice work. A heavily descriptive piece, the author does not make an editorial comment until the very end. Only then do we learn what she has taught us to expect, that the woman is about to die. The final reflection is poignant and compelling. (TH)

Stephen Gripkey
College: Yale University

Beyond salvation in this world, she lay slowly dying on a cheap mattress, her emaciated frame almost incapable of movement. A victim of malnourishment beyond medical help, she lay in agony, not romantic acceptance. No music played in the background; no trumpets heralded her pain-filled exit from this world. No poets commemorated her in song. She was nothing more than a human skeleton, and yet she strained forward to mutter greetings to a visiting nun. I watched for a moment, and then turned and strode away, gripped with oblivion. I felt no true shock or pain, or even sorrow; I felt only numbness and emptiness. I could not even cry.

During my summer-volunteer service in the Dominican Republic, such horrible sights of malnourishment and sickness taught me the dispassionate brutality of human life. I saw babies who are crippled for life because a $2 box of nutritious oatmeal came too late to save their weak limbs . . . decrepit mendicants who spend an entire day begging so that they may face another day of slow death . . . and children who have no hope for the future and only pain and suffering in the past and present.

When I was capable of having one, my reaction to such sights was anger. I was not angry with God because such people are allowed to suffer, but angry with man. We Americans have enough capital to feed the entire world, yet gluttony prevents us from doing anything.

And what of education? Philosophy, literature, classics, music—all are worthless to a starving man. Have you ever tried to explain the theory of relativity to a jobless man with eight children to feed? Or the laws of motion to a child without functioning arms or legs? All our technology and knowledge mean nothing if we are not prepared to use them to end such needless human suffering. Philosophy and knowledge can only be appreciated on a full stomach.

As for me, I intend to use my education and skills to help put an end to such suffering. Granted, the goal is probably naïve. But as Robert Browning once said, "Ah, but a man's reach should exceed his grasp. Or what's a heaven for?"

Juliet Siler
College: Harvard University

My brother Tommy died when he was four and I was six, so I never knew him well; however, I do have certain definite memories of him. Although two years younger than I, he was much stronger, built like a bulldozer, or at least a small ox. I was a scrawny coward in those days and he would chase me unmercifully, head lowered and a glint in his eyes—he had light hair and his grandfather's intensely blue eyes—and I would cry and he would laugh and get spanked and laugh even louder. He was fearless in the pursuit of his sister. Yet deep down, he admired me very much, more than I appreciated at the time. Whatever I was drawing, he would want to draw; whatever game I was playing, he would want to play, too. He always wanted to be with me, and he would enlist me in his own games, assigning me the American toy soldiers and himself the British. He never stopped moving; he was either energetically chasing me or running his toy cars along the floor. In all of his photos he is grinning his toothy widest, happy, ready to conquer worlds of bandits and bad guys, a cheerful little hurricane.

A lot changed when he got sick with leukemia. The illness sapped his energy and happiness and often led to fatigue and crankiness. Chemotherapy made his hair fall out and he had to wear a brown wig that didn't at all resemble his shining, golden hair. His fearless and trusting nature was—must have been—assailed by unspeakable bewilderment and terror. Yet he managed to smile when he saw me, laugh at television cartoons, and run his toy cars along the sheets. In his own childish way he was making the best of his life. Near his death, he asked my mother if there would be toy trucks for him to play with in the sky. She answered yes, and I know she is right.

COMMENTS:

This is a very affecting piece of writing. Without being overly sentimental, it invites an emotional response. In the process of learning a great deal about the writer's little brother, we learn a great deal about her as well. The vocabulary, the sentence structure, and ordering of ideas all contribute effectively to the overall impression. There is a great deal more I would like to know about this particular writer, and I expect that those matters would come clear elsewhere in her application. In any event, this piece does a good job of making clear one particular facet of her personality. (RCM)

A well-written description of Juliet's brother. I get a glimpse of her compassion and hope, but not much else. The essay is so focused on him that she gets blurred out of the picture. (AAF)

ESSAYS ON
FAMILY

Angelique Henderson
College: New York University

"Visiting hours are from 3–4 and 6–8."

The room was dimly lit and wherever light did shine, it only did so sparingly. He stood there, in that white, ghostlike gown that draped down to his ankles. Standing only feet away, it was still as if I couldn't see or touch him, only worthy enough to admire his unfamiliar 5'5" silhouette. He didn't appear to recognize me much either and instead gazed at me like a stranger he was seeing for the first time. Still, his eyes were both calling for me to help him and leave him alone at the same time. He is my brother.

How could your own brother not recognize you? My best friend asked me this question and all I could say at 10 is, I don't know. The answer didn't change much when I was 11, 12, or 13 either. The only thing I did know was that my brother had been diagnosed with bipolar disorder and had to be admitted to a mental ward at least twice a year since.

The whole circumstance puzzled me. The days, weeks, and months added that I spent at different wards from 3–4 or 6–8 on these occasions left me with many unanswered questions. Why my brother? What exactly is this condition? But most importantly, how am I to study or concentrate on anything when I have a brother who doesn't recognize me some weeks then sits beside me at the dinner table other weeks and asks me about school?

Now that I am 17 years old, I have acquired enough knowledge on the matter to make some sense of the situation. My brother suffers from extreme mood swings. "Well don't girls have that, isn't that called PMS?" I asked my mother that at 14. The answer was no and when I witnessed my brother pace back and forth through the house, then cry, then exert hostility to all those who came in his path whether it was parent, sibling or police officer, I knew why the answer was that way.

I suffered bipolar with my brother even though I don't have it. When his mood swings were occurring, I was there. When he was in the mental ward, I was there. When he didn't recognize me, I was there. I've spent so much time there, hiding from him, crying, visiting mental wards, questioning and answering, and now I want to learn. Learn all that I can in the life span that I am given about everything that I can. Now he is 22, takes his medication regularly, and is doing pretty well . . . and I'm still here. Now I want to do pretty well. I've always been here and now it's time to be where I'm destined to be, at my own mental ward called college. The patients there are cured and released after the acquisition of special letters like B.A. or M.A. I know where I'm supposed to be now.

COMMENT:

This essay has it all—it's a five-star essay in a three-star world. The grip of an opener, the hook pulls the reader in, the journey starts with a child's voice (very useful tool, I might add) and transitions into a young adult's. The writer flings the doors open to her family and invites the reader into the sideshow, knowing the spectacle to be seen is normal life for her. The writer shares the command her brother has over her life, how she managed to rise above, how this has shaped her path and acquiesced there is chance it can all crumble. The writer is exposed and vulnerable while still maintaining innocence. I would hand this back to the writer with the words "thank you" and wish her all the best. (BLB)

Meghan Elizabeth Brooks
College: Williams College

Having moved eight times by the age of twelve, I find that my childhood houses and neighborhoods have blurred into an unrecognizable Alice-in-Wonderland sort of place made up of jumbled rooms and landscapes. There is one place, however, which I know as soon as our minivan crests the hill above the beach. It is the summer hamlet of Humarock.

Coming down the hill I watch out the windshield as we cross the bridge my brothers swim from at high tide. At thirteen I finally summoned the courage to jump in myself, but a brush with a dead fish on the way down convinced me never to jump in again. We drive by the clubhouse where I spent Tuesday night socials hoping someone would ask me to dance and turn onto the street where my Papa first let go of my two-wheeled bicycle. I flew down the pavement, ecstatic, and then hit sand and skinned my knee. We pass the beach and then the car stops in the gravel outside my grandparents' house. Looking up at its yellow shingles I remember forts in the sunroom and naps on the hammock, and nights of dancing in the kitchen instead of washing dishes. Everything here is familiar and warm, from the splintering backyard fence to the red plastic rinsing tub. I know every inch; I can't remember when Humarock wasn't home, though soon, it won't be. My grandparents are selling the house. Yet, sitting here behind the windshield, I have made a vow not to let this place fade like the others. When I was younger and we moved from state to state, Humarock felt permanent. I now know nothing is. Maybe though, if I try, if I drive through Humarock enough times in the window of my mind, the memories will last.

COMMENT:
Wow, this essay immediately caught flight, hooked and did not disappoint. The first line pulls in the reader, questioning why did this

child move so much? At the end, it doesn't even matter. Speaking from a child's ambiguous view of the world, it moves to a memory the writer has chosen to secure. The essay shares social class, family, dealing with loss, coping with change and insight. The writer is moving into the world of an adult. It "sticks" on the first read. (BLB)

Anonymous
College: Harvard University

TOO EASY TO REBEL

In my mother's more angry and disillusioned moods, she often declares that my sisters and I are "smarter than is good" for us, by which she means we are too ambitious, too independent-minded, and somehow, subtly un-Chinese. At such times, I do not argue, for I realize how difficult it must be for her and my father—having to deal with children who reject their simple idea of life and threaten to drag them into a future they do not understand.

For my parents, plans for our futures were very simple. We were to get good grades, go to good colleges, and become good scientists, mathematicians, or engineers. It had to do with being Chinese. But my sisters and I rejected that future, and the year I came home with Honors in English, History, and Debate was a year of disillusion for my parents. It was not that they weren't proud of my accomplishments, but merely that they had certain ideas of what was *safe* and *solid,* what *we* did in life. Physics, math, turning in homework, and crossing the street when Hare Krishnas were on our side—those things were safe. But the Humanities we left for Pure Americans.

Unfortunately for my parents, however, the security of that world is simply not enough for me, and I have scared them more than once with what they call my "wild" treks into unfamiliar areas. I spent one afternoon interviewing the Hare Krishnas for our school newspaper—

and they nearly called the police. Then, to make things worse, I decided to enter the Crystal Springs Drama contest. For my parents, acting was something Chinese girls did not do. It smacked of the bohemian, and was but a short step to drugs, debauchery, and all the dark, illicit facets of life. They never did approve of the experience—even despite my second place at Crystal Springs and my assurances that acting was, after all, no more than a whim.

What I was doing then was moving away from the security my parents prescribed. I was motivated by my own desire to see more of what life had to offer, and by ideas I'd picked up at my Curriculum Committee meetings. This committee consisted of teachers who felt that students should learn to understand life, not memorize formulas; that somehow our college preparatory curriculum had to be made less rigid. There were English teachers who wanted to integrate Math into other more "important" science courses, and Math teachers who wanted to abolish English entirely. There were even some teachers who suggested making Transcendental Meditation a requirement. But the common denominator behind these slightly eccentric ideas was a feeling that the school should produce more *thoughtful* individuals, for whom life meant more than good grades and Ivy League futures. Their values were precisely the opposite of those my parents had instilled in me.

It has been a difficult task indeed for me to reconcile these two opposing impulses. It would be simple enough just to rebel against all my parents expect. But I cannot afford to rebel. There is too much that is fragile—the world my parents have worked so hard to build, the security that comes with it, and a fading Chinese heritage. I realize it must be immensely frustrating for my parents, with children who are persistently "too smart" for them and their simple idea of life, living in a land they have come to consider *home,* and yet can never fully understand. In a way, they have stopped *trying* to understand it, content with their own little microcosms. It is my burden now to build my own new world without shattering theirs; to plunge into the future without completely letting go of the past. And that is a challenge I am not at all certain I can meet.

COMMENTS:

This is a good, strong statement about the dilemma of being a part of two different cultures. The theme is backed by excellent examples of the conflict and the writing is clear, clean, and crisp. The essay then concludes with a compelling summary of the dilemma and the challenge it presents to the student. (NA)

A masterful job of explaining the conflict of being a child of two cultures. The writer feels strongly about the burden of being a first-generation American, but struggles to understand her parents' perspective. Ultimately she confesses implicitly that she cannot understand them and faces her own future. The language is particularly impressive: "It smacked of the bohemian," "subtly un-Chinese," and "a fading Chinese heritage." That she is not kinder to her parents does not make her unkind, just determined. (TH)

Lydia Bassett
College: Harvard University

Family legends passed down through generations grow more incredible each time they are told. Sitting at my grandmother's feet listening to her tell of my great-great-grandmother, Kate Travis, I knew *that* story would never change. The ideal of it was too important to be stretched and exaggerated, too important to be tampered with for the sake of a happy tale.

My great-great-grandmother was born an enslaved person in about 1845. She lived in a small, rural community, Horse Pasture, Virginia. She was allowed to keep part of her wages and when she was freed she had money saved to buy a restaurant in nearby Martinsville. With freedom a great desire to succeed came to Kate Travis. Money was not the important part of her dream. She wanted to raise her children with pride. She wanted them to be educated and have a chance to become what they wanted to be.

The restaurant was a success. Two of Kate's children died of small-pox. Her remaining son, Raleigh, went to school and grew up into an ambitious young man. But the dream of Reconstruction was dying. Martinsville was changing; Kate was constantly being hounded to sell her restaurant. There was no place for Raleigh there. With high hopes Kate traveled North with her son to help him establish a business in Chicago. She returned to Martinsville to find that Jim Crow laws had become more oppressive. A sturdy partition was constructed down the center of the restaurant and she was forced to run a segregated business.

Kate learned to live within the new laws, but that was not enough. Close by the courthouse, her land was desirable property. A victim of legal manipulations and her own illiteracy, she finally lost her restaurant, forced to accept as compensation land on the outskirts of town. Raleigh returned to Virginia, his ambition crushed. Chicago was not what he had dreamt it to be. He died, leaving a baby daughter for Kate to raise. She earned a living working as a cook.

I wish I could have known my great-great-grandmother in her later years, her bitter years. I would tell her that her dreams were not lost, they lived on in her granddaughter, my grandmother, who grew up into a woman with the same strong convictions as Kate Travis.

COMMENT:

Direct, strong, and simple, the style here reflects the content. She takes a family legend and without sentimentalizing it or politicizing it; without editorializing she takes the reader back in time and tells a story. She does exactly what she says. She doesn't "tamper with the story." The end works because it brings the story into the present and suggests themes of continuity, continuation, and generation. (PT)

Kelley P. Borden
College: Barnard College

> Somewhere ages and ages hence:
> Two roads diverged in a wood, and I—
> I took the one less traveled by,
> And that has made all the difference.
> —Robert Frost

I have chosen to take roads less traveled by. I have chosen to be different than other members of my family.

My family is one of backwoods heritage—down-to-earth, good-hearted people who value hard work and integrity. We did not step off the farm until my parents' generation, and then, only for economic reasons. In the past, members of my family chose to take the downtrodden path, the safe, well-known highway traveled by their ancestors. Some, I am sure did not have a choice, but others I believe chose the familiar path out of fear. I understand this fear, for I too experience it. It is a distrust of the new and of the different. My curiosity, however, helps me to overcome this fear, it entices me to look for bigger things and not to be content with what I already have.

Throughout my life I have chosen less traveled roads. I chose the road of an artist, the road of a dancer—a choice requiring hard work and total dedication, things family and friends do not always understand. While it causes me pain that my father does not approve of this choice, it has also taught me responsibility, independence, and survival.

Another road I decided to travel was that of a scholar, a path tough to walk on and easy to be pushed off of. Again it is an option which few of my family members and friends understand or dare to take. Peers pressure me to step off that path and follow theirs. Admittedly, there are times, especially in this past year, when I succumb to the pressures and walk off of that path. Yet, I know not to stray far for good things lie ahead for me on the road of scholarship. The door to a world better than one my parents are living in. This is what I am fighting for.

So far the roads I have traveled have been rocky, I guess because they are the less traveled, the lesser understood roads. Yet, I continue to travel them knowing it is worth the risk and the heartache, for one day it will all be rewarded. In many ways I could even say I already have. Dance has brought me the joy of movement and the freedom of self-expression. Scholarship has given me knowledge, an open mind, and a new perspective on life.

I do not condemn my family for not helping me down roads different from the ones they would have liked me to take, I just hope one day they will understand my choices.

COMMENTS:

This writer took a risk in writing this essay. It comes across a little negative—she obviously does not have her family to support her in this venture. On the other hand she is very open about herself and her goals even though she has "traveled the road less traveled by." She demonstrates her independence and determination to succeed on her own. (BPS)

There is a sort of churlish self-aggrandizement in this essay, which leans, too heavily in this writer's opinion, on Frost's beautiful poem. It would have been far more effective had Ms. Borden separated her positive vision of her life from the lingering hurt and resentment of her parents whom she cannot stop accusing. (SAB)

Ellen L. Chubin
College: Harvard University

MARLENE

I have never before attempted to collect and write down my thoughts about my sister and her effect on my life—probably because it's so difficult for me to talk about—but as I turn it all over in my mind, I begin to see what a profound impact she has had on me.

Marlene, now age twenty-two, was born with learning disabilities and a lower than "dull normal" I.Q. that to this day prevent her from functioning at a normal mental capacity. When she was first tested, her I.Q. was found to be 60% of an average child's, and though she now tests at 85% of normal, she continues to have severe gross and fine motor coordination problems, reading and speaking difficulties, and poor rhythm and balance. She is destined to remain socially and academically backward despite her efforts and those of my entire family.

Those efforts have been tremendous ever since I can remember, and I am told that they appeared even more shocking and unrelenting before my birth. When my parents initially realized that Marlene's unresponsiveness and lethargy signified mental handicap, they suffered a crushing blow that threw my mother into a severe mental depression, but they were determined that Marlene should reach her potential no matter how limited it may be. Throughout Marlene's life my parents have always sought out the latest information, techniques, and educational opportunities available for the learning disabled, and as a result of these efforts combined with her willingness to engage in the struggle to achieve, Marlene has made slow but steady progress toward emotional and intellectual maturity.

She began her formal education in private schools for the mentally deficient, switched to special education classes in public school, and progressed to a mainstream academic program in high school. Though such success might have been ample for the family of another L.D., Marlene's education did not end upon the receipt of her diploma. My parents again endeavored to find the seemingly unthinkable option for their mentally handicapped daughter—a post-secondary educational opportunity—and they discovered one. Marlene became a member of the first class of the two-year Threshold program—a specially designed college experience for high school graduates with significant learning disabilities—at Lesley College in Cambridge, Massachusetts. Upon graduation from Threshold, she entered the third-year transitional program to aid her with her full-time job in child care and her independent living arrangement in a Cambridge apartment with another Threshold graduate.

Though I do not spend nearly as much time with Marlene as I once did, we continue to share a close, caring relationship. When we were younger, our relationship was surprisingly mutually beneficial on the whole. The many things I tried to teach her in more recent years, after my accumulated knowledge had far surpassed hers, are balanced by the direct and indirect aid she gave me as a young child. Rather ironically, it was Marlene who first taught me how to read and write when I was two and three years old. She was seven and eight years old at the time and had just begun to develop these skills herself, but my parents verify that she imparted to me her knowledge in these basic academic areas through playful use of her educational books and toys.

I am also grateful to Marlene for a significant occurrence in my life which she indirectly brought about. My parents' hunt for a special summer camp program for Marlene led them to the Tikvah program at Camp Ramah in Palmer, Massachusetts, and my sister's first summer there was so successful, both socially and educationally, that consequently I began attending Ramah. This camp aroused my interest in Judaism and equipped me with the liturgical expertise that enable me to serve as a cantor several years later.

Now Marlene lives with two other Threshold graduates, works as a stock girl in a Boston department store (since our realization that she could not succeed in day care, though Threshold had trained her for such work), has a steady L.D. boyfriend, and relentlessly maintains a nearly independent existence, except for the continued support of family, friends, and hired social workers and other professionals. I wish to assist her as she struggles toward independence, and attending Harvard University would enable me to do so.

Marlene has taught me to be the best that I can be because that is what she is. Her kind, generous disposition has not become embittered by her endless battle in life. She has had to overcome so many more obstacles than the average person in order to satisfactorily perform ordinary tasks, and she continues that struggle although she knows she will never be totally successful. In that sense the struggle is hopeless, but she never stops—she never gives up. She is fighting the unbeatable foe. If she can achieve that much, can I be any less? I have to live up to her standard.

John R. Trierweiler
College: University of Michigan

My mom and I have played Scrabble for twelve years. We have challenged each other to over three hundred games; not once have I been able to beat her. In my house Scrabble is not just a fun little game that we play to pass the time; it is a battle for intellectual supremacy.

In second grade, my mom beat me by at least 150 points every time we played. Merciless in her routings, she often reduced me to the brink of tears. Yet, she insisted that all of the losses would help in the character-building process. I had no fear; I knew that as years of schooling increased, my mom's margin of victory over me would slowly dwindle. As I flew through sixth, seventh and eighth grade, the victories did get smaller. By my eighth grade continuation, I consistently came within 75 points of her score. Though the lead was still sizeable, I knew that my middle school years had made me a more enlightened Scrabble player.

High school was a letdown. My rate of improvement slowed dramatically. Despite the massive number of vocabulary words I studied while preparing for the SAT, I gained little ground. Even after junior year, my mom dominated by at least 60 points each match. The lack of improvement was very disappointing, but perhaps the most heart-wrenching moment came no more than a month ago.

The game started with my mom jumping out to a 45-point lead after two turns. I had almost given up hope, when I suddenly had a rack full of all the right letters. On my next turn I played "quartz" on a triple word score. My mom countered with "cat" for only three points. I then played "joggle" on a double word score, and with that, the 45-point deficit was quickly erased. If there was such a thing as the "zone" in Scrabble, I had entered it. The game continued with me attaining a significant lead. I began to think that maybe college was not necessary; I had already reached the highest level of Scrabble enlightenment. At last my ten years of Scrabble education had paid off. The good letters kept coming in, and I was confident that it was my turn to take over as Scrabble champion. By my last turn, I had opened up a 135-point lead. With fewer options, I played "hat." My lead now a seemingly insurmountable 138 points, my mom studied her last, futile move carefully. After more than fifteen minutes of pondering, I noticed the look of puzzlement on her face slowly turn into a smile. Adding to an "s" she slowly put down her letters one by one. My face twisted with horror as I stared at the board in disbelief. She had spelled "zebrulas" with a double word score and the "z" on a triple letter score. She had used all seven letters, which meant that she also received a 50-point bonus. "I win," she said with a smile and walked away from the table. I put my face in my hands and tried to hold back the tears.

College is my only option now. It is impossible to think that I could make up a 60-point deficit in my senior year. A college educa-tion is the only edge my mom has on me, and I believe that attending a prestigious school like the University of Michigan would prepare me well for my quest towards Scrabble greatness. Using all of the University of Michigan's fantastic resources, I would not rest until I was confident I could overtake my mom. Well, on second thought, I might take the occasional break on a fall Saturday afternoon to go and watch the nation's greatest football team march towards another victory at The Big House.

zebrula—the offspring of a horse and a zebra

COMMENT:

This is a light and comical essay about the writer's yearning to go to college so that he can eventually beat his mother at Scrabble. Ever since he was a child, he has been unable to do so; recently, he came close, only to lose big-time in the end, when the mother spelled a formidable word and won again. The problem here is that while the essay has a certain charm, it's one big joke. The writer never gets serious. I get no sense of what really matters to him, or why this particular school would be best at providing it. (MR)

Julia D. Kyle
College: Princeton University

IN THE BARN

To the casual observer, my family might have seemed fragmented. My older brother Josh and I lived with our mother in Philadelphia. My two younger half-brothers, Allan and Kent, lived with their mother in the small town of Pipersville. The four of us spent every weekend together with our father, who lived in a nineteenth-century farmhouse near Doylestown. The farm hadn't been worked for decades, but the huge, slightly decaying barn still stood.

Whenever I think of my childhood, that barn looms large in my memory. Adults almost never went in there. I think they were a little afraid of it—and with good reason, too. The floorboards had rotted in some places, and unless you knew exactly where to walk, you risked falling through onto the concrete area below which had once housed the cows. In some rooms, ceilings were half caved in, and the superstition developed among us children that if we spoke above a whisper in those rooms, the ceilings would fall in on us.

But for the four of us, the barn held more than fear. Sometimes the barn was awe-full, almost holy. We would stand quietly in the still of the afternoon and watch myriad particles of dust glitter in the rays of the sun that slanted through the cracks in the walls. We could hear the almost inaudible creakings and moanings of beams which had held together for a century and were trying to last yet another day.

Sometimes the barn was interesting. Josh (whom we considered omniscient) would tell us how farmers used to build without nails, show us barn swallows' nests, or explain how bats can fly without sight.

Sometimes it was challenging. Josh would lead us on expeditions to the top of the rickety silo, or to the uppermost windows which could only be reached by creeping precariously along the beams.

Sometimes it was terrifying. We would go into the barn at night and tell ghost stories. Some, I later found out, were well-known, like the Tell-Tale Heart, but the ones that still send a shiver up my spine were those we created just for ourselves. I remember one dark night when the wind was blowing through some wire, making a high-pitched wailing noise that sounded like demented laughter. The story that night was about four children (three boys and a girl, of course) who were killed, one by one, by the barn. Each time, just before it killed the next child, the barn started laughing. After that, whenever the barn "laughed," we would remember that night.

My father moved to another house several years ago. The barn has been boarded up so "children won't wander in and get hurt." Josh has married, and we're all too old now to be frightened by ghost stories. Yet sometimes we drive past the barn and those memories flood back, and I know that inside its crumbling exterior, the barn holds a part of us intact forever.

COMMENTS:

This is an excellent essay. I don't know if the essay hints at the character of the writer or whether she'll do well in college, but she should do well in a writing course! (BPS)

Brava! Julia, Princeton would be lucky to have you. What beautiful tension is created here, what understated home truths are revealed by the barn! This is a writer. She is also someone who manages to reflect in a way that is fiercely independent. She is truly transcendent and, best of all, she writes so well that instead of having to take her word that she is a writer the readers know it to be true. (SAB)

Deanna E. Barkett
College: Harvard University

When I was younger, I used to silently pray that I was nothing like my father. He was so serious. His brow was always knit. My grandmother could not remember a time when my father had done anything wrong. He was too perfect. I felt timid and self-conscious around him.

My father was always offering advice by which he swore. Although they may have been ancient proverbs or old adages, they were always "Daddy originals" to me.

"When you're prepared, you'll never be scared," he would tell me when I was up late studying for an evil chemistry test.

"Haste makes waste," was his rejoinder when I would bring home a math exam littered with careless mistakes.

"When you lose an hour in the morning, you search for it the rest of the day," is the Chinese proverb I learned on more than one Saturday morning of a weekend filled with homework.

"Live by foresight, learn from hindsight," he would say when I was younger and only old enough to relate "fore" and "hind" to the legs of a horse. These sayings interminably buzzed in my ear at times when, as I got older, I wanted to scream: "I know, Dad! You've only been telling me these things since I was two years old!"

I never elevated my father to sage status. I always recognized that he wanted me to do my best, but his advice lacked a loving tone. Indeed, at times his became a voice of nagging monotony.

As I have grown older, however, I have realized that Dad—in his own way—has these many years been trying to guide me. The denouement of my father's motivational speeches occurred this summer. I was away at summer school for two months in Massachusetts. It was the longest separation I have had from my parents.

Communication with my family consisted of more e-mail messages than telephone conversations. My father corresponded with me more than anyone else. He always returned my e-mails promptly and tried in his own silly way (he signed one of his e-mails "love ya!" which is not at all like my father) to make me laugh. So much so, I was reminded of another of his sayings, "When you lose your sense of humor, you lose your mind."

Near the end of summer school, Mom told me that Dad had printed all of my e-mails and was planning to take them to the family reunion. "You have pleased him so much, Dee. He is so proud of you and loves you so much," she told me. I had an epiphany: In my messages, Dad was reading about preparation and patience, time management and foresight. I made him laugh a lot too. Then I remembered another of his sayings, "The apple doesn't fall far from the tree." And I cried.

COMMENTS:

This is a nice essay about a young woman and her dad, and it has refreshing features, including the way the writer sets the tone in the introduction. Her short paragraphing style makes the piece readable and gives it a structure that helps it flow logically and coherently.

While she talks about her dad lacking "a loving tone," she ultimately realizes the significance of those "Daddy originals" that have come to guide her in her life's encounters. It is effective, and not all essays about dads can deliver this kind of smart, moving conclusion that is not maudlin, despite the tearful resolution. Her reflection about her father's true wisdom, and her own affection and respect for him, make for a strong conclusion. (RK)

Ron Lee
College: Harvard University

As far as I could tell, Ted Williams, Dom DiMaggio, Walt Dropo, Birdie Tebbets, Billy Goodman and all the rest came from humble backgrounds. On that basis I used to think there was some connection between rough childhoods and good batting averages, which is why I sometimes wished my own house would burn down, to give me an edge.

—Laurence Sheehan
"How to Play Second Base"

Things I will always remember about my family: my father showing up for soccer games in out-of-the-way places; my mother driving me to a Little League practice she really didn't want to go to; doing my homework at my desk and being interrupted by my sister who comes in, lies on my bed, and talks with me while "You know?" and "I know," go back and forth like a responsive reading in church . . . I will leave all these things next year. No matter where I go to college, I will never again be with my family as much as I have been—as much as I would like to be.

Dad started coming to soccer games when I played freshman soccer. He stood on the sidelines, alone, and watched the game attentively, hands clasped behind his back. I never told him how to get to a game; he just showed up. When I left the field at the end of a period, he would call me over with his hands. Not quite sure of what he was talking about, he always said the same thing, "You're playing good, Ron. Bend your knees a little more. Are you tired? You look tired." I would utter some witless remark and respond to his comments by bending my knees more and running harder when I got back in the game.

When I was eleven, my mother came to visit me at Boy Scout Camp. I knew everyone else's parents would be there, but I was still comforted by my mistaken belief that my parents weren't coming. Looking back, I realize how touchy I was about being the only Korean, the only non-white, at the camp. Undaunted by any of the self-consciousness that burdened me, Mom showed up with my sister Michelle, Kentucky fried chicken, and some things to help me through the week. She did not embarrass me with her poor English, as I was sure she would. My mother's confidence and love made me ashamed of my own unfounded insecurities. I am thankful to my family for giving me a sense of identity in being Korean, something that has proved to be a blessing, not an embarrassment or obstacle as it has been for other first-generation Korean-Americans I have known.

Now and then Michelle will say with a sigh, "God, Ron, you're going to college next year." I respond with a forlorn "I know." I have gotten an "edge" in exactly the opposite way Laurence Sheehan hoped he could: I haven't had a "rough childhood"; God has blessed me with an amount of talent, but as college draws near I realize He has blessed me with a family I will miss a great deal.

Recently, I have realized how profoundly a child is shaped by his parents and his environment. My family has helped me to become secure, appreciative, confident, and independent. If I am accepted to Harvard, perhaps the letter of acceptance should be addressed to me and my family.

COMMENT:

It's a poignant conclusion. Again what works here is the use of specific examples. The closing makes the "sincere" tone authentic. (PT)

Kimberly D. Morgan
College: Harvard University

GROWING UP ON THE JERSEY TURNPIKE

"Howard, slow down, you're tailing that blue car!" We switch lanes. "Danielle, move your leg!" demands one voice. "How much longer," demands another.

This is common banter on my family's frequent drives to New York. The route to my grandparents' house isn't "over the river and through the woods" as in the stereotype of Americana; but over bridges, turnpikes, and highways. In fact, their house isn't even a house; it's an apartment. Once every six weeks or so, my family makes the pilgrimage to a far off land called Queens, New York. The journey takes over three hours and although it is usually an ordeal, it allows me to spend a significant amount of time with my family. We have been making the same trip since I was about three and it has become a family tradition of a sort, and one which I have found myself looking forward to.

The first fifteen minutes of the drive is always crazy. My mother worries about how late we will be while my sisters and I fight over our seating positions. Then the inevitable battle begins: the war between the radio stations. It is the "Sinatras" against the "New Wavers." Eventually an armistice is called and a compromise is reached. The "New Wavers" may have their station until it is overtaken by static and then they must relinquish control to the "Sinatras" for the remainder of the ride. Oddly enough, the static appears after about 45 minutes and we are stuck in a car with the big band sound.

We have also developed our own rules and regulations for these rides. The most important ones govern food. The "Constitution" is as follows: no pretzels until the first toll booth, two cookies each while in Pennsylvania, and the rest must be divided equally after we reach the N.J. Turnpike. Most importantly, NO throwing trash on the floor.

Usually after we have passed exit 7A (the one for Great Adventure) and we've divided up our snacks, my sisters fall asleep. This is one of the best parts of the trip for me. For an hour or so I am an only child. I lean over the front seat and turn off Frank, abruptly ending "That's Why the Lady Is a Tramp."

"So where am I going to college?" "Wherever we can bribe them to take you," teases my father without missing a beat. Lately all of our discussions seem to concern college. Where do I want to spend the next four years? What interests should I pursue? What are my long-term goals? Although it is hard to admit, talking it out with them has helped me to focus on the sort of experience I want for my undergraduate years. Essay topics also take up a lot of our time. What is there about me that distinguishes me from the thousands of other bright Harvard applicants? "Emphasize leadership," suggests my father, taking both hands off the wheel to gesture. "Make sure you mention the grant," adds my mother. "Just don't mention the trips to Europe," they add in stereo.

"Why don't you tell them that you always wear my clothes without asking." My sisters wake up and again, I am part of a trio of girls who strive to spend equal time fighting and having fun. When we pass Newark, we all talk in nasal voices as if we were holding our noses. We do the same thing when we sense a skunk near Cranbury and when we drive through Secaucus. We play the alphabet game and twenty questions. And, when we reach the Elizabeth exit, my sister declares, "We are now going through the town with the most awesome name in the world. Mine!" While passing a service area we note its obscure name. "Who the hell is Richard Stockton?" "He was a New Jersey signer of the Declaration of Independence," answers my father, the world's authority on everything.

The ride continues. We see ships at the piers in Brooklyn and keep up our quest for unusual license plates. In my fourteen years on the turnpike I have spotted all except Alaska. We cross the bridge, see the abandoned car that's been in the same spot on the B.Q.E. for thirteen months, and finally hit Queens Boulevard. The green sign for Lefrak

Towers is the signal that it's time for the socked feet and footless shoes to become one. As the car circles the block for a parking space we rapidly gather our belongings. When all is in place my father ceremoniously declares, "We're here!"

Our car rides are really a microcosm of our life together as a family: teasing, advising, arguing, joking, and caring. Some of my funniest moments, loudest discussions, and soundest advice have been shared between the tolls of the New Jersey Turnpike. Perhaps it is because I have taken so many comfortable car rides with my family that I can now travel to college as an inquisitive, confident, eager person armed with humor and a realistic sense of self. Now, if only I could convince the "Sinatras" that New Wave is the REAL music those trips would be truly worthwhile.

COMMENTS:

Wonderfully irreverent, honest, and observant! Underneath the pull and tug of family life there is a sense of bonding: of "teasing, advising, arguing, joking, and caring." She should have resisted the temptation to draw the too obvious connection between the family and college, but it was probably her father's idea. (TH)

I *like* the essay, for sure. I've driven the route myself often enough. But the essay is too long for an application, I think. It sustained my interest because of my familiarity with the route, and I wanted to compare notes with her. She has a great feel for her family and conveys it well. The phrase "for an hour or so I am an only child" is quite poignant, and many of her quips are quite cleverly expressed. I reacted negatively to the use of "Who the hell . . ." and wonder if "B.Q.E." is comprehensible as such. Overall, well written and interesting. (MAH)

While the essay is well written, and there is depth, it tends to labor along the turnpike. There is almost a travelogue quality about the essay. To her credit there is a definite sensitivity and family being which comes out. (JCM)

William S. Plache
College: Haverford College

When my brother, Alex, was in law school a few years ago, he lived at home with us. But he always did his studying at my grandma's house. He said there were fewer distractions and he could concentrate more on his work. So after several unsuccessful attempts to write the great college admissions essay at home, I have decided to see if I can do any better over here. Instead of using my own desk at home, I am sitting at Grandma's kitchen table.

I came over alone this time, as I usually do lately. But I can remember when our whole family would go together to see Grandma. The holiday occasions when we would all come for dinner are still vivid in my memory. Christmas Eve at Grandma's house was an annual event. Just getting there was an experience in itself.

My father would make it clear to the whole family that we were to leave our house by five o'clock. But as it turned out every year, he and I were the only ones ready to leave at that time. Dad was always on time, and I had nothing to do to get ready. The youngest didn't have to get dressed up to go to Grandma's, and nobody expected him to wear a tie. The others, however, were in a mad rush to put on their formal outfits.

Finally, when everybody was ready to leave, at quarter after five, we would all pack into the Citroen. Our positions in the car were pretty well established. Dad always drove. No matter where we were headed, Dad was behind the wheel. Next to him, in the passenger seat, was my mother. The back seat was left for the four boys. Alex, Dave, Matt, and me. Darwin proposed his theory of the survival of the fittest, and such journeys were no exception to this idea. I always ended up in the middle of the back seat, forced to contend with the hump that runs along the floor. As the youngest of them all, I never thought of complaining.

The first moments of our ten-minute trip were filled by the harsh yet familiar lecture of my father. "For crying out loud, Marilyn, I said we had to leave by five. We're a half hour late!" Over his shoulder, he would exclaim, "You always wait until the last minute to get ready! Why can't we ever get anywhere on time for Pete's sake?" Nobody cared to mention that we were not a half hour late, but rather only fifteen minutes late. And dinner would not be ready until six o'clock anyway.

The rest of our drive consisted mostly of silence, except for some occasional jostling in the back seat, which was immediately extinguished by the emergence of Dad's proverbial hand of discipline reaching around from his own seat.

When we arrived, Grandma was busily at work in the kitchen. Mom would stay to help mash the potatoes, while we went into the other room to wait. The dinner was always great, but what I looked forward to was the dessert. Every year Grandma makes thirteen different kinds of Christmas cookies, and when she brought them out, we would each grab our favorites. After dinner, we all assembled in the living room, where Grandma had her artificial tree set up. I would eat one of the candy canes that were hanging from its branches. Then Grandma walked in bearing six envelopes, one for each of us. I opened mine to find a fifty-dollar bill. Alex would shout, "A hundred dollars, thanks Grandma!" We all anticipated this annual quote, and we knew that everybody's gift was equal.

Today, as I sit here it is quiet except for the sewing machine Grandma is using in the other room. The Citroen broke in half ten years ago, and has been replaced by a succession of odd cars over the years. Alex, Dave, and Matt have all moved out. They visit occasionally, but they are never all home at the same time, and when they do return, their wives usually tag along. Grandma still makes her famous cookies, but she has to mail them to her out-of-town grandchildren.

COMMENT:

The beginning is promising, but his memories are not well tied to his present task nor are they particularly unusual. It bothers me that the only emotion expressed is anger. (JMcC)

Jacob Press
College: Harvard University

Sunday was the day we went visiting. Just about every sun-baked, suffocating, summer Sunday during the period known as my childhood, extending as far back as I can remember and rapidly coming to a close, we packed ourselves up in the car and drove down to "the Beach House," my grandparents' summer home.

This weekly pilgrimage was not simply a trip, like a drive to the shopping mall, the butcher, or the Chinese restaurant. It was nothing less than a journey to a different culture, like a weekly student exchange program. Gone were the elaborate landscaping and fancy cars sunning themselves in driveways. Here there were no driveways and, as you gazed up, it was obvious that the trees had been here long before the people. All the homes on this street were similar: small frame houses with large front porches and shingles that had once been shiny and bright but were now faded by the saltwater air into softer, friendly pastels, so that no matter what color a house might have been when it started out, it eventually fit in perfectly with the others.

It was the same with the people. They had entered this block as independent individuals, but over time their facades, like those of their houses, had faded together. As they aged together they became closer, and a community was formed where the phone wasn't used to call neighbors who were just a short walk away and one could drop in next door for dinner unannounced (and frequently did). The women shared recipes and the men shared financial advice and they all joined in the powerful and mysterious cult of the Grandchildren which, through its powers, forced otherwise rational people to swear that their five-year-old grandsons were taking college-level classes.

The drive was just long enough to be massively miserable, but was immediately forgiven as we drove up the street and spotted Grandpa waving hello. He must have been waiting on the front porch for hours, but time meant very little to this octogenarian. My Grandpa was a slight, short, usually quiet gray man. He preferred bow ties, and gave perfect hugs: not very powerful, and not lasting very long, but covering you from head to toe with a feeling of well-being that made you feel at home. I've been told that in his day he had quite a temper, which I find hard to believe, but if so, he had certainly mellowed. He took just about everything in stride, including Grandma, which was quite an accomplishment.

We would all make our way inside and shortly Grandma would come trotting out of the kitchen, drying her hands on the apron that covered her stout, slightly plumpish body. She seemed always to be washing dishes, in spite of the fact that she had owned a dishwasher for a number of years. She "rinsed" the dishes before she put them in, explaining that it was absolutely necessary. In a loud voice she greeted us all, gave a hug, and said, "So, why are you so late, you said you would be here at twelve?" as she took some packages and my mother back to the kitchen. "Sam, I think you should go warm up the barbeque," she shouted across the house, "it might need some new coals. Kids, you won't believe how cold the water is, I couldn't even put my feet in. On Wednesday, Aunt Pearl and Uncle Herman were here and they were saying, well actually Aunt Pearl was saying, Herman wasn't really paying attention, so what else is new, Pearl was saying that she remembered that the water in Florida . . ." Grandma was rarely at a loss for words. Whether on line at the baker's or on a bus full of strangers she had enough to say for everyone, but especially her family.

So it was to these warm surroundings we went in the warm

weather. Little did we know that we were being filled with memories of people and an atmosphere that were almost extinct. These visits helped me understand much about what a community should be, what a family is, and where values and priorities should be placed. No matter what I do or where I go, I will always keep these Sundays in mind. And maybe someday young children will come to visit me in my beach house.

COMMENT:

This is well written. When given a choice, write about that which is known or familiar. This is written about a childhood experience that obviously left a deep impression on the writer. (BPS)

Leah S. Schanzer
College: Swarthmore College

WASHING UP

Recently my grandfather showed me a photograph of my grandmother when she was just eight-year-old Eva Littwin, living a little girl's life in post-World War One Brooklyn; she stands in the courtyard of a tenement building, hanging laundry to dry (perhaps this is her regular Monday afternoon chore, and when it rains, are the wet sheets and underthings hung in the kitchen, to drip and run in thin rivers over the linoleum floor? On rainy Mondays, does my great-grandfather joke that dinner is cooked at sea?). Smiling roundly, she holds a grubby dish towel before her stocky little body with a dainty turn of wrist, as if it were a heavily draped evening gown.

During my own eighth summer, my sister and I established a tradition of eating breakfast with my grandparents Eva and Max. Each morning we would race across the wide lawn which separated our house from our grandparents', nightgowns flashing about our legs, night-tangled hair flying straight behind, to trip onto the wet, cold flagstone path which led directly to their front door. The first thing my grandfather always did when he got up was to turn his radio on to a classical music station—the memory of that announcer's voice, gentle and without inflection, as familiar as an old friend, was a great comfort to me in my times of eight-year-old trouble.

My grandmother always made my grandfather a single fried egg, sunny-side-up, and served it to him in a heavy old cast-iron frying pan, while my sister and I looked on in distaste: It was our job to do the washing up. As soon as breakfast was finished, we hurried to clear the table, for we usually liked to be quick as possible, and very efficient. But sometimes, if it were a rainy day and Bach spoke to me eloquently from the speakers in my grandparents' bedroom, I would put the sponge to one side in preparation for my special Sink Dance.

My grandma's nylon Peds became beautiful worn toe shoes which transformed my feet into the strong, bony feet of a dancer, and conjured for me the breathlessness of a dancer's life. My sink dance was an expression of what I felt looking around at the smiling faces of my sister and my grandparents, there in that summer kitchen—lifetimes of experience. Urged on by Bach and the steady, quiet rush of tapwater beneath, my dance took me across rooms, around corners, careening and leaping through the whole house. When it was all over, my sister giggled knowingly, but my grandparents always kissed me and told each other, low, that I was a graceful girl, wasn't I?

Afterward, I was ready to get to my chore. I could appreciate the feel of the musical water running over my hands, and I squeezed liquid soap onto the sponge with a will as I looked out the little window above the sink at the bright sodden flower beds my grandma had planted long ago to line the walk. Beside me, in companionable silence, my sister stacked everything in the drainboard and when we were through, we stood back to admire the way the dishes slouched orderly, gleaming, against one another. Just as eight-year-old Eva Littwin must have admired the rows of sheets and dish towels which billowed and danced on their line in the tenement courtyard.

COMMENT:

It's very atmospheric, and I like very much the first part of the opening paragraph and the closing. There's a lovely sense of the way generations echo each other. What is particularly good are the images. They are concrete and emotive. I thought the weakest part was the parenthetical section in the first part. (PT)

Brittany Krupica
College: Wheaton College

YA YA'S HANDS

Dry, scaly, cracked, yellow stained hands. These were the first vivid images that came to my mind when I thought of my grandmother. For more than forty years, those hands had given birth to hundreds of thousands of "Marsh Wheeling Stogies." These were my Ya Ya's hands.

Standing outside, I gazed at the breathtaking sky that hovered above my mountaintop West Virginia home. Glowing in the east were sinister clouds, moving ever so slowly across the vast sky. The whole sky was alive with clouds of ever-changing shapes and colors, from steel blue to crimson red. It was the sight of my beautiful surroundings that had first sparked my interest in wanting to become an international environmental lawyer.

The dark, desolate grey houses, built during the coal mining struggles of the 1920's, stood tall in the dismal shadows of the clouds, providing a sharp contrast, while the numerous puddles reflected the radiant colors peeking through the rain clouds. Sweet thoughts began to transfix my mind about my friend, my teacher, my inspiration. It was a picturesque scene; however, the thoughts of my dear grandmother were more vivid than the beautiful countryside of West Virginia.

It has been nine years since my grandmother died, and still to this day I can remember the distinct smells that filled her old, wooden-framed house. For as long as I can remember, my grandmother smoked cigarettes. Etched deep within my memories of her is the description of her hands. Her long, bony fingers reminded me of the bare winter branches of an oak tree, sprawling out, desperately reaching toward the sunlight. As the days passed on, I watched my grandmother's health fail. Cancer had begun to take over her body. Sadly, I had to witness her agonizing deterioration.

Since the death of my grandmother, I have taken an active stand against cigarette smoking, especially with youth in West Virginia. Alarming statistics give evidence of West Virginia's tobacco-induced cancers. Teen smoking is rampant and truly distressing.

Last year, I was Chairman of the Ohio Valley Health Awareness Organization. As Chairman, I led ten area high school students who participated in the volunteer organization on various research topics regarding tobacco-induced cancers. Our group presented our research to fifty oncologists from the Wheeling–Pittsburgh area. The biggest impact was our presentations at various schools in Wheeling.

Our enthusiasm about encouraging youth not to smoke prompted interest among local television stations. I worked diligently to organize public service ads that warned of the dangers of teen smoking among West Virginia youth. The 2000–2001 "Ohio Valley Cancer Research" team was a big success (despite all the time constraints and countless meetings for preparation), and today I continue to promote a tobacco-free youth society throughout West Virginia.

As I sit here now, gazing at the morning sky, I am contemplating my future. My grandmother has instilled in me the values of love, compassion for others, and most important, the gift of generosity. I am enthusiastically awaiting my journey to college, for I want to continue following my passion of volunteering.

I have a vision, a lofty ideal in my heart, to make a positive impact on the world, to make a difference, for the next ten, twenty, or forty years from now. Someday, I will return to the beautiful state of West Virginia where I will continue my work as a professional. I don't want West Virginia's youth to grow up blanketed by smoke. Instead, I want them to be embraced by the radiant colors of the Appalachian mountains. I want them to be inspired by the breathtaking vistas, and meandering crystal-clear springs, and roaring rapids.

Recently, my passion for preserving the beauty of my surroundings led me to organize an environmental project at Harvard University's Summer School 2001. By encouraging the cleanup of Harvard Square, I was thrilled to receive help from more than twenty summer school students. Seeing Harvard Square a little cleaner was rewarding, but seeing the excitement and enthusiasm among the volunteers was equally gratifying. Community service is important to me and I hope to continue it throughout my college years.

My grandmother's hands were full of compassion and strength. I want to become a servant for the greater good. Like my grandmother always said, "People don't care how much you know until they know how much you care!"

COMMENT:

This essay begins with the painterly imagery of the writer's grandmother's hands, which she wisely references throughout the essay as she describes the poignant details of the grandmother's impending illness. From "radiant colors peeking through the rain clouds," however, she dramatically shifts her writing voice in the section where she "led ten area high school students" in a research project. While she speaks lyrically and idealistically about her return to "the beautiful state of West Virginia where I will continue my work as a professional," she perfunctorily describes her volunteer experiences. In the final paragraph, the cigarette-stained hands are now "full of compassion and strength" as the writer comes to understand her grandmother as inspiration and her own desire to "make a difference." Despite the shift in style, this connection, and the discussion of her motivation to volunteer, makes the essay stand out. (RK)

Susan Ashley
College: Harvard University

I clattered the habitual four plates onto the counter before remembering the need for the fifth. I held the smooth china, round, blue, familiar, then placed it in front of the smiling, foreign face. New hands ate with the old silverware that night and new accents graced our familial conversation.

Later, my foreign exchange sister and I sat together on her bed, recently moved into my room. Ozge unpacked the photographs and trinkets her closest friends had sent with her to America. I listened to her stories of her life in Turkey and her excitement to share my life here, in Nebraska. My cozy room, transformed into a cluttered mass of beds, suitcases, and chaos, reflected my own feeling of confusion. I, too, felt the thrill of the moment. How often does a girl meet her "sister" full grown and ready to embark on an adult relationship? However, on the fringes of my excitement, I began to sense just how enormously she would impact my life.

By October, I thought I had adapted to life as a younger sister. I kept my room neater, enjoyed less of my parents' attention, and delighted in the nonstop companionship of the girl who was quietly becoming my dearest friend. Not until March did feelings of resentment and jealousy begin to plague me.

I knew it was petty. My sister deserved all the attention she got, and my parents didn't love me less just because they also loved her. But like the child I still was, I couldn't overcome my anger. In my immaturity, I pulled away from her. I found fault with everything she did and I had no tolerance for her. I didn't want to spend time with her and more importantly, I didn't want my friends spending time with her. I wanted my own life back. I wanted to be everyone's obvious favorite, with no competition for my place.

For close to a month, I maintained my puerile attack. This fight embodied my maturation. My world had grown, and I had to grow with it. Day after day I faced a choice: continue persecuting the Turk or swallow my unfounded jealousy and beg for forgiveness. As a grown woman, I loved her and wanted her love in return, but as a child, I could see her only as a threat.

I knew I had to resolve the struggle alone. I lay awake through the night, arguing with myself. In the early morning, I slipped out of bed and tiptoed through the dark room. I paused at my desk, the dividing line between her side and mine. On my side, I was a child, but when I crossed the line, there was no going back. With a sigh of courage, I plunged across. The moon peeked from behind her cloud, illuminating my sister's silent face. I caressed her cheek, and she moaned contentedly. Gingerly, I crawled into her bed and we awoke the next morning, clasped in each other's arms.

COMMENT:

This is a well-crafted essay with an intriguing first paragraph. Through artful prose, the writer quickly opens herself up to the reader as she communicates candidly her ambivalent feelings about her "sister, the Turk." Struggling between the woman and girl within, the writer takes a risk, exposing her immature and "puerile" reaction to her "sister's" popularity. The frankness about her jealousy and resentment lends dramatic emphasis to her moral dilemma. In a surprising conclusion, the writer evokes suspenseful curiosity as she reconciles her inner issues, crossing the line unexpectedly into womanhood. Though the skeptical reader might view this essay as contrived, the writer's refreshingly concise statement more likely is a risk-taking venture in self-disclosure. (RK)

Michael Wechsler
College: Harvard University

I have often thought that the fictional character Hawkeye, the lead role in the popular television show M.A.S.H., is based on a "real-life" individual: my grandmother. What—you may ask—does a gentle, gray-haired little lady, who is more familiar with the layout of her kitchen than with the battle zones of Korea, and whose skill is with knitting needles rather than with a scalpel, have in common with the sardonic, perennially unshaven, lanky surgeon of the infamous 4077th army unit? The answer is character; the strength and nobility of character that manifest themselves best under conditions of adversity, which made their presence felt, and which leave a lasting impression.

Like Benjamin "Hawkeye" Pierce, my grandmother has had a war against which to rage. In fact, she has had many: the two World Wars spent in Eastern Europe, experiencing inhuman conditions, unimaginable horrors, and senseless losses; later the struggle against poverty and hardships that faced her as a new immigrant to America; and more recently, the long personal battle against an illness that has confined her to a wheelchair. But, for both the fictional character and his living prototype, the raging is simply the manifestation of an indomitable spirit, of an unwillingness to accept as unsurmountable the problems created by the madness of human conflict or the unpredictability of fate. Both have been successful in tempering this rage and channeling this frustration into positive, useful action. Both have survived with dignity and earned the affection and respect of those around them.

The prime moving force for each is a fundamental love of life, with an enormous capacity to care for others. Hawkeye spends his time patching up fragmented bodies with his sutures and encouragement. He risks his life on numerous occasions to save his comrades and patients; she has always placed the well-being and happiness of others above her own needs and desires. Even now, despite her infirmity, she does volunteer work regularly, teaching arts and crafts to severely handicapped adults. What does it matter that he comforts his friends with homemade gin and a pat on the back, while she uses homemade chicken soup and a hearty hug? The common bond is the willingness to take the time to give of oneself, to stop and alleviate the misery in someone else's life.

Both Hawkeye and my grandmother consider frankness of paramount importance. Forthright and outspoken, they will stand up for a belief, defend a value, or protest an injustice. In the same way that Hawkeye does not hesitate to challenge an unreasonable order or a corrupt decision—even one emanating from a general—my grandmother has not shied away from questioning the excessive rigidity of an official regulation, or from objecting to the prejudicial treatment of a minority group. He does not tolerate the abuse of a subordinate; she has taken the cause of the elderly and handicapped, and fights for their rights.

The ability to laugh and to make others laugh is another attribute they share. Endowed with a superb sense of humor, they are quick to dispel a gloomy mood or defuse a moment of tension, raising the most flagging of spirits. They have a knack for detecting the absurd in affectedly grandiose situations, for deflating pomposity with a subtle jest, and for disarming anger with a wink and a smile. It is this ability that has allowed them to deal more easily with the crises and disasters of life, for the poking of fun extends to their own predicaments: ready to receive the anesthetic prior to her seventh major bout of leg surgery, my grandmother extracted the promise of a dancing date from her handsome young physician. Hawkeye, who flirts with the nurses to hide his fear of loneliness, would have understood, and rushed to hire the band.

The fictional young doctor from Crabapple Cove, Maine, and the very real eighty-year-old lady that I love share many qualities: sensitivity, warmth, compassion. Having experienced my grandmother's gentle care, I readily recognized the tenderness with which Hawkeye looked after a pet hamster; watching Hawkeye's tears on witnessing the suffering of a friend, I was reminded of my grandmother's gentle sorrow under similar circumstances. Their touch has made a difference in many lives.

To me they represent the essence of being human.

COMMENTS:

The writing here is of a high order. The vocabulary is excellent, and so is the sentence structure. Most important, the comparison of Hawkeye and the grandmother works, from beginning to end. The similarities are clearly delineated and effectively supported with examples. Learning about what he admires in these two characters tells us a good deal about the writer himself. (RCM)

Although his last sentence lacks the punch I expected, this student draws an excellent parallel between his grandmother and Hawkeye Pierce. He joins two unlike persons into harmony by skillfully describing their common attributes and values. His insight and sympathetic portrayal of his two models indicate a strong appreciation of the values a person of intelligence, wit, and moral perspective would cherish. I believe it is a self-portrait. I like him! (AAF)

OFFBEAT AND OTHER ESSAYS

Anonymous
College: Wellesley College

Sitting in my doctor's office, I vaguely heard the distant remark, "You're so thin you could have a heart attack while walking down the street. Don't you care?"

No. As I ran my index finger along the cave between the blades of my pelvic bones, all I could think was how revolted I felt at the thought of my former weight. My doctor's remark did not affect me, for I feared food a thousand times more than I feared death. During my ninth-grade year, I suffered from anorexia nervosa. After taking fifty-three pounds off my five-foot nine-inch frame, I was left with ninety-six pounds. It was not enough to be thin. I had to be the thinnest. Now, however, fully recovered, I can reflect back and realize that my wishes were more complex than fitting into size five pants. Many of my subconscious emotions were related to my relationship with my father. I hardly knew him because as I was growing up, his work always came first; as he often left the house before six in the morning and came home after eleven at night, I would not see him for up to two weeks. Not only did he devote his whole self to his work, but he expected me to do the same ("You cannot get anywhere unless you go to Yale or Harvard"). Consciously, however, I never felt pressure to please him, nor did I miss a close father-daughter relationship. But it never occurred to me to recall that I began dieting after the first time he told me I looked fat; always in the back of my mind lay that element of trying to please him, to achieve a goal that would earn his pride, and to do it better than anyone else.

Games were for winning. I played starvation. Society urges us to stay slim at all costs, but many people have trouble restricting the size of the number on the scale. I could: I was a winner! I compared myself to my classmates, people in the street, and, of course, my hottest competition, the *Vogue* models, who always beat me. But Daddy knew I was struggling to win; with every shirt that became too large for me, his remarks went from sincere compliments to anxious threats of punishment if I did not eat. He noticed me.

At the time, however, I had no awareness of those underlying emotions or desires to achieve for Daddy. All I knew was that I had to be skinny; skinnier than anyone else. Every month or so my father went to lecture in Europe for a week or two and on the days he left, sorrow and emptiness consumed me; Daddy was leaving. But I just considered my feelings—"the blues." I also enjoyed a mysterious frail, helpless childlike emotion that came from starving. I liked to know that I needed to be taken care of; maybe Daddy would take care of me.

Now, two years later and thirty-eight pounds heavier, I realized that I cannot alter my father's inability to express his feelings. Instead, I must accept myself. I finally realize that I am a valuable person who strives to accomplish. But I cannot strive solely for others. By starving, I attempted to gain pride in myself by attaining my father's approval or acknowledgment of my value as a person. Of course, I gladly accept applause and attention from others, but the primary approval must come from me, and I feel secure now that I can live with that knowledge safely locked in my mind.

COMMENTS:

This strikes me as a gutsy piece of writing. Anorexia is a hard rap to beat, and the writer is entitled to feel proud of the fact that she has. Furthermore, she describes the struggle in compelling terms. I wish it had been possible for her to do so without making a villain of her father—perhaps because I am a father myself—but no doubt that is an important part of her story. It seems to me that the essay fulfills the two basic requirements for such writing: It provides significant information about the applicant as a person, and it clearly demonstrates that she is able to write effectively. (RCM)

The essay avoids what could be the inevitable pitfall: self-pity—or, even worse, a maudlin description. As a reader my strongest reaction was to examine in my own life who it was that I was seeking to please. Rather than focus on the anorexia problem, the writer effectively describes the reasons at the basis of the problem. The cognitive explanation was so insightfully presented along with the writer's affective reaction that they result in a very successful outcome. The reader comes to know the author very personally. (AAF)

Sarah H. Bayliss
College: Harvard University

WHY I WEAR UNDERWEAR

I yanked open the top bureau drawer. No underwear, only tube socks, wadded into tight balls and packed in. I now owned seventeen pairs of tube socks and six pairs of underwear. The washing machine had a habit of "eating" my panties. I reached my fingers into the back of the drawer, finding only emptiness where my last-resort pairs were usually stashed.

"We're leaving in ten minutes!" my older sister Alice shrieked from the kitchen as she did every morning.

After selecting a pair of socks, I shut the drawer and tugged open the next two. I took out my orange corduroys and my green-and-purple striped sweater. I pulled the first over my bare bottom and the second over my uncombed head.

"Coming!" I shouted back. Snatching up my unfinished third-grade homework, I dashed into the kitchen.

My sister, dressed in a denim shirt and clogs, looked at her watch five times as I gulped my cereal.

Barbara was playing jacks by herself outside the music room during recess. Her round hazel eyes were flecked with bits of brown, and tan freckles spilled across her cheeks and nose. She was in fifth grade and was a friend of Alice's. I decided I was going to look like her when I got older.

"What's up, Shrimpo?" she said as I snuck up behind her. I was planning on "boo!"ing her, but she saw me first and twisted my arm.

"Uncle!" I gave in after a few moments, and she released me. I hadn't realized my elbow could bend that far without breaking. The joint creaked as I straightened my arm and tried to laugh.

"There you are!" a husky voice boomed from the other end of the hall. It was Lisa ("Obesa"). Her toothy smile made me shiver.

I said, "Oh, hi."

"Why weren't you outside the lunchroom? I told you to meet me there!"

"Um. I forgot."

Lisa had flabby white arms and pierced ears. She always wore complicated earrings which, combined with her abundant wavy hair, made her look enormous.

"Well, that was dumb," she said. She stepped behind me, pressed her palms on either side of my chin, and picked me up by the head. I kicked the air until she set me down again.

"We'll just have to give her a wedgie then, won't we, Barbara?" Wedgies involved being hauled up by the back of one's underwear. Lisa's eyes glittered; her sausagey fingers reached for me again. She locked my neck in the crook of her elbow. I threw Barbara a pleading look. She answered me by gripping me around the waist and pulling up my sweater in the back. Her fingernails tickled my spine as her fingers crept downward. As I struggled, I was held up again by the head.

"What's the matter? Aren't you wearing any underwear?" Barbara joked and grunted as I elbowed her in the stomach. I would be destroyed if they got down my pants and found no underwear. I would have to switch schools. I sweated through my gritted teeth and thrashed my arms. Squeezing my eyes shut, I squirmed as hard as I could. Someone ripped my belt loop. My arms, swinging in wild rotations, smacked into something. I kept swinging, twisting, squirming, striking . . .

Suddenly, Lisa unclamped. Still kicking, I landed on the cold tiles. When I unshut my eyes, she was clutching her nose and facing the door to the girls' bathroom. She turned around slowly. At her feet, a pool of blood was collecting from her dripping nose. Riveted, I stared at Lisa's bloody face.

A bell rang. My fly had come undone. I zipped it up and tore down the hall.

I ripped my new sheet of arithmetic homework in half.

"Hey, Shrimp!" My sister sounded excited. Her voice came from the other side of my bedroom door. I blew my nose and tossed the tissue on the Kleenex-littered floor next to my bed.

"What!" My locked doorknob jiggled back and forth.

"Why'd you give Lisa Obesa a bloody nose?"

"I din't!"

"We saw her in the nurse's office! Everybody knows about it." She giggled and whispered something I couldn't understand. I heard Barbara's muffled voice cackle in response. I wouldn't tag along with Alice and Barbara today. I decided not to look like Barbara after all.

"Well, I didn't mean to!" I walked over to kick the door.

As Alice's clogs clomped off, I crumpled my homework and hurled it at the wall.

Later that evening I noticed that someone had shut my top drawer. I opened it and found four new packages of Carter's underwear tucked in among the socks.

COMMENT:

The reader gets involved in her childishness, her embarrassment, her struggle. She handles the ending sensitively. It has a nice pace and rhythm and fine structure. (JMcC)

Paula Bernstein
College: Wellesley College

LESSON IN SELF-EDUCATION

"Identify these quotations from *Hamlet*," read the instructions. My stomach tightened my palms sweat. "Calm down. This is only a test," I reassured myself. I was in English class surrounded by twenty grim-faced students who were busily pouring ink onto their papers while I watched the tree through the window grow and the hands on the wall clock tick-tock.

My eyes raced down the page. "Hamlet said this to Ophelia during the 'Nunnery Scene' . . ." I thought to myself. I knew the answers, at least some of them. But time was fading and my classmates' heads continued to sag and the tree continued to grow into the sun. I began to identify and explain one of the quotes before I stopped myself. "You could write a great poem on this moment. Taking a test. Watching robots suffer to achieve. Seeing the sun shine on the carpeting unnoticed. Not wanting to explain what I know. Wanting to write . . ." So I did.

"Carpe diem," explained my English teacher in a previous class, "means to seize the moment." So I did. I turned over the test and wrote a poem about Hamlet, me, the tree, the clock, and why I felt the urge to write a poem on the back of my test.

"This can't be your test," my usually placid English teacher said in an unusually harsh voice as I handed the test to him. "No, that's it," I replied, trying to repress a grin.

My teacher called each of us to his desk about a week later to tell us our grades. "I already know what I got," I said to him. He smiled ear to ear and said, "I have no doubt that you do." "Well, did you at least enjoy my poem?" I queried. "Yes," he replied. I explained why I wrote it and why I felt that it was a legitimate reason to leave a test blank. "I felt that it was something I had to do, something I had to prove," I explained. He agreed halfheartedly with my excuse. "But," he argued, "you should be able to write poems *and* take tests." I knew he was right, but at that moment something inside me seemed to laugh at life and although no one appeared to notice, my eyes seemed brighter, my cheeks seemed rosier, and I seemed to strut proudly through the halls the rest of the day.

I only regret that my teacher lost our exams before he could hand them back to us. I keep thinking that someone at this moment may have my Hamlet exam with an "F" on the top and a limited edition poem of mine on the back.

NOTE: This essay was written in response to a question asking my views on active learning and risk-taking in education.

COMMENTS:

I find this a weak last paragraph for the essay. It doesn't help me to sympathize with the type of "risk-taking in education" she's written about. The earlier paragraphs don't build my confidence in her academic values either. I don't think this essay was as helpful to her as it might have been—it wasn't helpful to me. (MAH)

Very nice. She writes about something we all would like to do. Succinct, serious, witty—all with a purpose. We are able to identify with the writer. Also, we see the serious side to her, in a short span of time. (JLM)

Matthew Brady
College: University of Chicago

I love small children. For the past three summers I have worked as a counselor at a playgroup for children from three to seven years old. Kids at that age are both sweet-looking and incredibly rambunctious. Each weekday that the children were left off at the Convent of the Sacred Heart in Manhattan, two teachers and I looked after them. It was my responsibility to keep the children occupied and out of trouble, not an easy undertaking as we had just a classroom and a rooftop on which to play. I invented games for them that would employ their imagination, told them stories, and tried to avoid being their punching bag. I enjoyed my work so much that, starting in my junior year at Exeter, I became a volunteer teacher's assistant at the local Montessori school. My duties there vary from those in New York in that I also act as tutor to individual preschoolers. Whether it is helping them learn to pronounce the alphabet or to count up to twenty, I receive such pleasure that I look forward to each Tuesday morning session throughout the week.

My experience with small children leaves me with more than good feelings; from my dealings with them I have equipped myself with some basic rules and observations, called Brady's Laws for Understanding the Young:

I. Kids always say it's theirs when it isn't (i.e., cookies), and claim it's not theirs when it is (i.e., a mess).

II. The ability of kids to do as they're told is inversely proportionate to the number of kids in the group.

III. The worse you feel, the friskier they act.

IV. The brattiness of kids is directly proportionate to the number of weeks he joins the group.

V. The smaller they are, the louder they shriek. Corollary: The louder the shriek, the harder they fall.

Finally, the short but true realization:

VI. The cuter they are, the harder they hit.

I know this early wisdom will be helpful to me when I have my own kids; I'd like to continue to work with small children in some capacity during college.

COMMENT:

The essay section does not necessarily tell us that Matthew is a highly skilled writer, but perhaps that can be revealed elsewhere. I find "Brady's Laws" to be quite clever—in my estimation the best part of his answer. *This guy does know about kids!* A rather informal style (use of the word "kids," frequent use of abbreviations), but this doesn't seem to detract from the quality of the response. The opening statement, "I love small children," is very direct and immediately wins me over to Matthew—especially when he is able to document that love by relating his involvement with "the kids." It would have been better had Matthew related details of his work with one or two individual children—to make his experience "come alive" to a greater extent. (RJO)

Adam Candeub
College: Yale University

I have been telling lies all my life. It's not as if my lies are malicious or even self-serving. I just like to test people's credulity with fantastic stories of my own invention which I am somehow able to tell with a very straight face.

I told my first fib in Sunday school at age five. I had ignored the teacher, and when she scolded me for not listening, I answered meekly that I was hard of hearing. My poor Sunday school teacher was moved with remorse and sympathy toward her disabled student, and afforded me special attention to make up for my disadvantage. Unfortunately, this idyllic state of affairs ended two weeks later in

Bonwit Teller where my teacher met my mother and asked her what was being done about my hearing problem.

My grade school friend, Neil, was fascinated by the very strange old lady who once lived in our house and honeycombed it with peepholes. They had all been sealed except for one which looked into my older sister's bathroom. Neil never came to my house without furtively inspecting the walls near that room. When after two years, I finally confessed the truth, our friendship ended, since Neil had no sense of humor.

I heard many lectures of the evils of making up stories and many renditions of that children's classic, *The Boy Who Cried Wolf.* These warnings did not prevent me from telling Todd about my maternal grandmother who played contrabassoon for the Philadelphia Orchestra or Amy about my pet parakeet, Louise, whose eggs we ate regularly for breakfast.

Junior High marked the creation of my greatest fib, my dear, beloved, and nonexistent sister, Adalgisa Candeub, named after the Druid temple virgin in Bellini's opera *Norma*. She attended Oberlin College where she studied art-anthropology and fell in love with the French art historian Thierry de Beauharnais, a direct descendent of Josephine, Empress of France. They lived in France where they researched the Neanderthal paintings in the Lascaux caves. When Adalgisa became bored with Thierry she ran away to the Antarctic with Haakon Lagerlof, a Swedish ornithologist. Together, they studied the migratory patterns of Emperor penguins on the Ross Ice Shelf. Mrs. Kaplan, the woman who used to carpool to tennis clinic, still inquires about Adalgisa's health whenever I see her and is amazed that she has yet to catch a cold in the Antarctic.

After Adalgisa I resolved never to fib again, but last summer at the University of Pennsylvania, while I listened to some students whine about their awful parents, the uncontrollable, creative impulse overwhelmed me, and off I went. I never see my parents, I told them. My mom, an archeologist, is always on digs in the Yucatan Peninsula; my dad does research on acid rain for the Canadian government in a lakeside cabin in Northern Ontario. I have to stay home with my evil guardian, Mrs. Crumbschurtz, a freelance artist, who designs the decorations on Dixie paper cups. She is so mean that I am only allowed out once every three weeks. These kids were aghast, and they invited me to live with them. That night my resident teaching assistant told me that if I wanted to discuss any personal or family problems, his door was always open.

Why do I make up these stories? My favorite English teacher once offered an explanation that appeals to me. According to her, storytelling is the first step to literature. The hallmark of any literary person is, therefore, an interest in stories. In any case, I no longer fib to people; I save my stories for my writing, and I would never lie about important things like college applications . . . honest.

COMMENT:

After eight years of reading "practice" application essays written by college prep juniors, I would have to say, this is almost the very best one I have read. My greatest sense of relief came in the last paragraph, when Adam admits to the motivation that underlies his fibbing. I believe that many readers would engage themselves with his works (fiction or nonfiction) in the future, because of the talent he possesses. Any individual who can tell five stories in one essay is extraordinary! (AAF)

Theodore Grossman
College: Brown University

At Home

What is written here is not what I had intended to write. I'm sitting in my home alone. My parents, my younger brother and sister, and our two dogs all packed their bags and went to our cabin in Wisconsin. They left me alone so I could work on my application. I was all set to really get rolling. I had a couple of friends over the night before to relax. And I went to bed early so I could get a fresh start in the morning. Only I had a foreign visitor in the house. A very good-looking dog. He had sat at the front door all day, howling. It was so cold at night I let him in. He crouched in the corner and went to sleep. When I woke up I gave him some food and let him out. As he had a collar, I assumed he had a home. Then I started thinking about all the things I could say in my essay which would typify Ted Grossman. But the dog kept coming back and sprinting away. Finally I let him in. He sat a couple of feet away and licked the snow from his feet.

We can't keep him. We have two dogs and my father barely tolerates them. I was going to take him to the Anti-Cruelty Society, but he should have a home, and so we will try to find him one.

The dog may not be the best thing to write about, but to me he's important. And this situation is similar to so much of life. Everything seems to be going somewhat on track and then a dog walks in. I only have a little time to finish this application and mail it. But how can I not worry about this dog? I could talk about all the reasons I'm so cool, and so bright and did this or that. But the fact is, that's not all of me. Aside from being the guy who dressed up as a girl, or played soccer, or edited the school paper, I'm also the guy who lets stray dogs in.

There is a passage from Sherwood Anderson's *Winesburg, Ohio,* which also captures some of my feelings. It's long, but here are a few of the lines: "There is a time in the life . . . Ghosts of old things creep into his consciousness. The voices outside of himself whisper to him concerning the limitations of life . . . If he be an imaginative boy, a door is torn open and for the first time he looks out upon the world, seeing as though they marched in procession of nothingness, lived their lives, and again disappeared into nothingness. The sadness of sophistication has come to the boy . . . He wants, most of all, the love and understanding of others."

The boy in Anderson's passage may feel as though his life is meaningless. And at times it's impossible not to feel that way, and not to question life, and not to want a why, even where there isn't one. The dog reminds me that even though there are questions that can't be answered, there are other things in life that give meaning. And this helps me have confidence that I have the ability to excel and succeed, and should take advantage of life, however it comes.

In ten years college will matter more than the dog, and I know that. But I can't feel it, not now. Watching the dog, caring for him, I feel a sense of satisfaction and worth. That is more important to me than ultimate answers.

COMMENT:

Writing from the moment and in the moment can be dangerous. In this essay the appearance of the dog and the transition from the dog as real object to metaphor and symbol makes the essay work. The way he slides into the quotation from *Winesburg, Ohio* was wonderful! (PT)

Sam Liu
College: Harvard University

You strain to be able to see just one more line of the chart sitting twenty feet in front of you as if your fate depended on it. "Z!" you cry out confidently, but what is the next letter? Is it "C" or "G"? By now your eyes are sore from squinting. It is no use. You resign yourself to your destiny, telling the doctor, "I can't see any farther." You are myopic, destined to be among the one out of every four people in need of glasses.

At the age of fourteen, I was brought to an optometrist because I could not see the blackboard. I had always assumed that what was fuzzy to me was fuzzy to everyone. I discovered that I did not see the world as others did. "You did the wrong problems for homework again," my science teacher would tell me. He would then go over the correct problems on the board, which seemed to be miles away. I had my eyes examined, found that I was nearsighted, and received my first pair of corrective lenses.

Fiat lux! I was now Superman, with X-ray vision. There would be no more doing the wrong problems for homework, no more missing fly balls in baseball, and no more wondering why everyone thought that the girl who sat in the first row of English class was such a beauty. Spectacles opened a new world.

The reactions of my friends were mixed. Some thought that I looked rather handsome with glasses. There were those who were amused by the way the combination of sweat and gravity sometimes pulled the frames down my nose. On the other hand, other people did not like them. "The eyes are the windows to the soul." Is it right to hide behind glasses? Some complained that I looked different. The natural reply was, of course, that they looked different also: They were no longer out of focus.

When someone is said to be nearsighted, it carries negative connotations of being absentminded and unable to think ahead. However, this is not true. Naturally, people who must wear glasses sometimes have to put up with inconveniences. Protective goggles worn in shop class must be oversized to accommodate the extra lenses. One has to be careful in sports. (I find that basketballs have a way of "homing in" on spectacles.) There are always those who ask to look through your glasses. Obligingly, you hand them over, sometimes to be passed around through several persons. The glasses are often returned with the comment, "I can't see through these. You must be blind." This is due to the forgivable, but probably false, assumption that corrective lenses give a person with normal vision an idea of what uncorrected vision is like. In addition, after being handled by twenty pairs of hands, the lenses were usually opaque.

Strangely, some people have enjoyed the view through my glasses.

One friend has told me that he thought the world looked more "peaceful" through my lenses. There is the expression, "looking at the world through rose-colored lenses." Perhaps my friend was right. Can it be that myopia is actually a state of mind? (Could I but see myself as another sees me!)

Uncorrected vision has its advantages. As stated earlier, nearsightedness should not carry negative connotations. Nearsighted people have to get closer and are forced to examine things more carefully. In addition, there is a certain privacy to myopia. When I study, I do not usually wear glasses. There are fewer distractions.

Finally, much beauty arises from "imperfect vision." It has been speculated that Vincent van Gogh's fondness of yellow was due to a physical condition that caused the world to look yellow to him. Everyone sees differently. Who is to say what is perfect and what is imperfect? For example, the beautiful twinkling of the stars is caused by the atmosphere and our astigmatism. Otherwise, they would appear as drab, perfectly round dots of light. Some people see with their hands, ears, and other senses. These people have an added perspective that people with "normal vision" don't have. In the final analysis, "seeing" is a mental rather than a physical act. To see through another's eyes is to truly get into his mind.

COMMENTS:

The idea is original and well-executed, although a little long-winded. The descriptions are the strength of the essay—giving strong impressions of the person as well as the incidents. His sense of humor, sensitivity, and insight are clearly reflected. The essay leaves the reader with a sense of who Sam Liu is. (JWM)

An excellent, clever, sometimes humorous analysis of a common problem. The student uses basic but very adequately descriptive vocabulary. It is a well-organized, nicely developed essay that is presented from an apparently original perspective. (TG)

Scott Locke
College: Brown University

I went through a C.I.T. program this past summer which taught me how to work with children: teaching them to be independent, while learning how to grow as part of a group. During the course of the summer I grew attached to many of the children. This attachment was one of the most meaningful experiences of my life. I grew attached to one child in particular, because of this I hope to work with children often in the future. His name is Jason. Jason is only eight, but he and I developed a bond that is incomparable to any I've experienced with anyone else.

Jason and I developed a sort of symbiotic relationship that produced much more than either of us consciously put into it. He wanted someone older who would care enough to spend time with him. When I came along he was thrilled. In turn he offered his love and complete trust. This bond is very similar to that between brothers yet different in that it lacked the sibling rivalry aspect.

Through working with Jason I learned to accept responsibility for and to be aware of the needs of children. Jason's being only eight years old made him seem so innocent; he appeared to be vulnerable and I sought to protect him from harm in the way a parent would for his or her own child. Despite my good intentions there was one time when I failed.

I was coaching a baseball team on which Jason was playing. To convince him to play the outfield, I told him that his team needed him there. This was completely true. I must have "laid it on" a little too thick. When a crucial play came his way he was nervous and the ball rolled through his legs. This was followed up by a grand slam home run. By the time the inning was over, Jason was crying hysterically. He told me that he let "*me*" and the team down. When he said that, I felt rotten. To think that he was so worried about letting me down touched me. It was this feeling of affection that has made me decide to work with children in the future.

Recently my brother, who is a friend of Jason's brother, told me that Jason was upset because he hadn't heard from me and thought that I did not love him anymore. When I heard this, I immediately wrote to him telling him that I still love him and always will. When I learned that I had such a lasting effect on a child I was on a self high. I got such satisfaction knowing that I could bring joy to others and form a lasting bond of love.

COMMENTS:

Scott means well and probably does a lot of good. The problem here concerns both the writing style and the thinking. Both are clichés. Every upper-middle-class Counselor in Training wants to tell how he/she climbed the mountain. They didn't. They were pleasant and helpful. Unfortunately this piece aggrandizes all that. Using godawful expressions such as "meaningful experience" and "from this . . . I learned" our writer attempts to sanctify the trivial. (SAB)

This writer, while giving something of himself to others, really perhaps gained more than the children. The writer was asked to give the college more information about himself not shown on the application. The writer demonstrates through this experience his concern and sensitivity to others. Most colleges are looking for people who can relate to others and are not just scholars. (BPS)

Jamie F. Metzl
College: Brown University

I do not have a father on the alumni board of Brown, I don't even have an uncle there. All right, I was not elected to the presidency of some huge, national corporation. I can't (if you promise to keep it a secret) tell you of my Olympic trial in the javelin throw. (Probably because I've never seen one of those long, wormy things.) I do, however, have a seven-inch-tall plastic Godzilla.

Godzilla hasn't always been with me though; he was born and raised in the wilds of a Taiwanese rain forest. When he was only a small monster, his mother sent him for a dental appointment in Taipei. Godzilla, whose family was inbred (for obvious reasons), suffered from dyslexia. On his way, he passed by a large factory which had a sign reading LETTAM. Little did he know that this was his family's most feared spot. He was instantly grabbed, priced, and boxed for shipment. (Once his brother, who also had dyslexia, had wandered into a ship headed for SOIDUTS LASREVINU, but that's a completely different story.)

Godzilla was sent to the United States, where he was imprisoned in a shiny glass case for three years. Then came his emancipation; I bought him. I took him to his new home: my shelf. There he now proudly stands between books of Thoreau and Emerson, and Kermit the Frog.

Godzilla is not the tough exterior he portrays. The true Godzilla lies within. Through my interaction with this paragon of monsterness, I have come to understand his meaning. Godzilla was born in the wild, yet he was pulled away from this by the forces of society. He has never, and will never abandon, his natural view of the world. His truth is only what is true to himself, not to any toy company or movie studio, or anything else for that matter. He believes imposed truth to be a monstrosity.

Godzilla has been given a pretty bad rap by the press, but I'll be the first to admit that he's really a sensitive monster. This is because he has huge eyes which allow him to really look around. He wants to use this vision to understand as much of the world around him as possible, so that he can be honest with himself and not only be influenced by the immediate.

I have given Godzilla a new home, but even with this foundation, he is an eternal dreamer. He dreams of the ideal, of true beauty.

Once, when I woke up, Godzilla had done a strange thing. He had ripped a page out of one of my books of Thoreau. It read:

> If you have built castles
> in the air, your work need
> not be lost, that is where they
> should be. Now put the
> foundations under them.

Godzilla wants to be free to explore and strive for his dreams. To do this, he needs to be free from all but his own restrictions. He wants to use this freedom as a means of exploring himself, not only as a dreamer, but as a monster.

And so as I curl up in bed each night, I look over at Godzilla who speaks to me of myself. He speaks of truth, he speaks of understanding, he speaks of dreams, and he speaks of freedom. He also speaks of being a plastic-covered monster in the middle of the Midwest.

COMMENTS:

This essay is a thoroughly entertaining escape into the author's imaginary yet real world. The freedom, joie de vivre, and creative expertise the author reflects in this essay validate qualities that, I believe, are important to a college community. (AAF)

This is another offbeat essay that certainly achieves the goal of making the writer stand out from the crowd; and the juxtaposition of Godzilla and Thoreau is an arresting one. There is a certain amount of cuteness, such as describing a javelin as "wormy" and the monster as dyslexic. Some of the sentiments about truth, beauty, and freedom are a bit top-lofty, too. On the other hand, such ideals are a part of the dreams of youth, and the final sentence is quite simply a lovely change of pace. (RCM)

Eric Pulier
College: Harvard University

I've been offered advice for every conceivable situation. Relatives, friends, teachers, enemies, even strangers, have bits of wisdom to pass on to me. This is not to say I accept anyone's counsel lightly. I evaluate advice carefully before adopting it.

There is serious information that others have given me in the hope that I may avoid having to discover it for myself. In this category is the advice of my grandfather, whose last words to me were to live my life with hard work and honesty. I have no doubt of the merit of these sentiments, as he was living proof of their success.

Separating this class of advice from the less somber, such as my grandmother's, "Don't eat standing up or you'll get fat toes," is not as easy as it may first appear. Only after much experience can I now keep the different categories of advice apart in my mind, and even now clarification or further explanation is often needed before a final judgment is possible.

When I was younger, the very idea of questioning the advice of elders was foreign. When my mother was cold, she advised me to put on a sweater. Not until the sweat began to flow did I suspect that the advice might be flawed. Could it be that the thermal identity I had shared with her as a fetus had ended? The implications of this train of thought was staggering. I took off my sweater and told my disbelieving mother the reason. In this case the advice had not been offered for reflection but obedience, and she put the sweater back on me. The line that divides advice from rules is often indistinct.

Advice from strangers is quite easy to come by. My experiences with this kind of advice have taught me a great deal. There was the man who exclaimed, "Bet Silver Slew in the Fourth, kid, ya' can't lose!" Needless to say, I could. Then there was the stranger with the fantastic tip on Southern Pacific Petroleum stock. It seemed that the Iranian hostage crisis was going to create a demand for Australian shale oil. After I thanked him heartily and bought the stock, it plummeted to one-hundredth its value. The lesson is obvious: Ignore the advice of a stranger unless he's paying.

Advice on marriage is the most sensitive kind. Any objections to this advice are met with a flood of supportive examples. Marriage advice ranges from my parents' "marry the girl that you love," to my grandfather's "marry the Jewish girl that you love," to my grandmother's "marry the Jewish girl that you love who will wash your socks for you." As I said, some advice is not meant for reflection.

Unfortunately, a great deal of the advice I get is forgotten immediately and is consequently unavailable for further discussion.

Certain advice does lurk in my mind, however, and springs forth when I'm presented with an applicable situation. Notable is that of the wise old lady of the Teaneck Townhouse Scrabble Club, who spoke these fateful words: "Son," said she, "never use a bank for less than forty points."

COMMENT:

I like the way the student gets right to the point of what he wants to say. He has a one-sentence introduction that avoids too much flowery establishment of a thesis statement, and thereby is a welcome sight to committee readers already red-eyed. He comes up with clever, quite original witticisms ("ignore the advice of a stranger unless he's paying"), and the generally humorous tone makes for enjoyable reading. It tells us much about Eric in the process. Reading this I had the feeling I was watching a good stand-up comedian, who illustrated points of everyday wisdom with pertinent anecdotes—and whose next one-liner I awaited eagerly. The only criticism I would make is of the rather abrupt ending, which prevents the essay from concluding with true impact. (RJO)

Brian C. Smith
College: Pomona College

One Terrific Task: Just the Morals

The selection of a quotation with a special significance to me is a difficult task because I feel that I have to tell you everything about my hopes and aspirations in just a few lines. I consider myself somewhat more complex than that, so I decided to concentrate my efforts on a quotation which I believe has had a significant effect upon my moral development.

Quotation: Alice the Maid

Every boy's a man inside—
Every girl's a woman, too
C'mon take a lesson from Mother Na[
Here's what you've got to do

When it's time to change
You've got to rearrange
Who you are into
What you want to be
*Sha Na Na Na Na Na Na Na
    Sha Na Na Na Na
        *[repeat]

Perhaps before I begin to speak about this quotation I should familiarize you with its origin. This bridge and refrain, from a song originally performed by The Brady Six, are two parts of a terribly deep and deeply moving song I heard first on a television show of the early 1970s, *The Brady Bunch*. This show was (and still is for millions of others and myself) the story of a lovely lady (Carol) who was bringing up three very lovely girls. She, a widow, met Mike Brady, a widower, who was raising three boys of his own. Well, the one day that the lady met this fellow, they both knew it was more than a hunch, and were wed. Alice, the maid, and Tiger, the dog, rounded out the cast, and with a team of brilliant writers behind them, they produced the most winning combination of pointed social commentary and good ol' down-home fun this country's networks had ever seen.

They're Not Just Beautiful; No Panacea

The Bradys have given me many treasured memories, but their rendition of this song is the one I hold most dear. The simple, gentle, and loping lyricism of the song makes it aesthetically beautiful, and its traditional structural setting hides furtively the more important questions posed. The Bradys forced me to face the political and social upheaval of the times—the Nixonian presidency, the feminist insurgency, the self-centeredness of the generation, and the final disintegration of the Vietnam policy. Although I did not make it through this period unscathed, thanks to the Bradys I did not end up glassy-eyed and directionless. The Bradys possessed incredible foresight, but even they could in no shape or form offer a panacea to cure all the world's ills. They realized that both political and social change would be gradual, offering steps to follow so that change could come about ("Change . . . Who you are into What you want to be"). The Bradys were optimists, and they were extremely enthusiastic about what man could inevitably accomplish with the proper guidelines. Ever-changing man, when exposed to change, is capable of almost any task set before him. Practical methods need not be presented when the solution is this universal. Life is a far simpler endeavor with the Bradys leading my way.

True Solution Is Mine; Reach the Refrain

Do the Bradys offer the only quotation that encompasses all that my morals have been built upon? I give answer in this manner, "Yes, I say, Yes!" Most quotes I could disregard easily, their meanings being too distant from my inner self. Actually, the only two families other than the Bradys to whom I seriously gave consideration were the Kennedys and the Partridges. All three families dealt extensively with art and social consciousness, and both of these are of special importance to me. Yet, ultimately, I found their theories on life too reliant upon the upper classes dragging the rest of the world through man's progress, too pessimistic about the capabilities of your average "Joe." Where these two families can project only stagnancy, the Bradys have given the people of the world a chance at glorious triumph. For these reasons, the Bradys' influence on my person has been all-pervasive, they have made me a more complete individual.

COMMENTS:

An original approach although a bit lengthy—a good message from a bright, intense young man. It works because he writes well. (JWM)

This student expands well on an unusual "quotation," thus revealing his equally unusual choice of a model family. Although the writer touches upon what this show did for him I feel he could have gone into more depth to explain more fully the true effects the show had upon his life. (TG)

SELF-PORTRAITS

Ellen L. Beckerman
College: Princeton University

It is a very difficult thing, to define one's self on a piece of paper. Can anyone, through one example, reveal his essence? Whatever words I can grasp will never have the richness of the emotion they are meant to convey. On the page my words look hollow, inadequate: "beauty," "pride," "pain," the words do not hold the intensity of the actual feelings. The image may be there, but the feeling, the feeling must be experienced, and in each person it will be different. And whatever two hundred words I use will be scrutinized, will be ME in your eyes. How can I show you who I am in ten minutes when it has taken me every breath of the last seventeen years to even begin to ask myself the same question?

I am the honey-colored sounds of my grandmother's grand piano on a Saturday morning when the family has gone out for breakfast.

I am the scent of burning leaves and smashed pumpkin, and I am the foggy breath off the top of the pond next door.

I am the scintillation of colored city lights as the car cradles across the bridge, the skidding of windshield wipers across drizzled glass, the streaking of each light into lines of pink.

I am the smack of a spinning volleyball against sweaty forearms, the burning of elbow skin against a newly waxed gym floor.

I am the clean sting of chlorine and the tickle of freshly cut grass which clings to wet feet in summertime.

I am a kaleidoscope of every breath, every shadow, every tone I have ever sensed.

*　　*　　*

I went on a canoe trip and stood under a pine tree watching the rain patter against the lake and felt the warm summer wind and thought that I had found absolute peace and perfection in one droplet of water.

I sang at a school talent show for the first time in my life after years of being stage-shy. The crowd was small and cozy, and the light was warm as the guitar hummed. I ignored my fear, because everything was perfect, and let myself be free and sang and sang . . .

I don't know whether Ronald Reagan is good or bad.

People who argue that nuclear war is bad annoy me because they assume that someone on earth thinks that nuclear war is good, and avoid the real issue, which is how to prevent nuclear war.

I don't understand people who hate camping. I hope that I never feel that business and politics are more real than a pine forest or an open plain.

Reality and perfection are in my mind synonymous. I think that the word is perfect. Even things which I hate are perfect because hatred is no less real an emotion than love. Famine is terrible, war is terrible, murder is terrible. But to say that nothing terrible should exist is denying everything this world contains. There cannot be wonderful without terrible. Pain is just as beautiful as joy, from an objective point of view.

The exciting thing for me is that I know that there is so much more for me to learn, and that everything I embrace as truth now is a very small part of what I will eventually be able to recognize.

The terrible thing is that I know when I die I will not know a millionth of the knowledge which all people on earth collectively hold. No matter how many days I sit and read, research, engulf information, I will never be exposed to everything. And right now I want to be exposed to everything.

COMMENTS:

Philosophical, poetic young lady. The introductory paragraph is a bit histrionic; the next several reveal some beautiful appreciations and recognitions; the third from last is confusing. The last two are honest and genuine. I'd take her into my honors program. (MAH)

Absolutely wonderful. Insight, depth, expressiveness, clarity—all are part and parcel of this essay. Not only do we know the writer but we can understand her. P.S. Extremely well done! (JLM)

Jordana Simone Bernstein
College: Harvard University

This one has the right idea. He knows where he wants to be, and he is determined to get there, even if it means swimming against the tide. He might be forced to push past those in his path, but he seems sensible enough to do it gently, without disturbing the flow. He may not be making the best move, but he feels it is right for him, and that is all that matters. One cannot be sure if he is turning toward something or away from it, but there is purpose in his stroke and he has a goal. One hopes he will achieve it; he probably will.

Independence of thought is marvelous. With an idea and a desire to fulfill it, the possibilities are infinite. To develop such an idea, one first answers the basic question, "What is it that you like to do?" The response is a personal one, and in order to reply accurately, there is the need for exploration.

I am pleased to have been offered numerous opportunities to explore many different areas. There have been clubs to join, organizations to belong to, activities to participate in, and experiences to share. My greatest difficulty seems to be that I am interested in too many things for a twenty-four-hour day. I have learned to set limits for myself by developing a sense of priorities. I can only try to move in a specific direction, aiming toward a goal while continuing my investigation along the way.

Although he is only a Pepperidge Farm goldfish, the depth of his message is greater than the paper he is printed on. This creature makes a subtle and important statement. His individuality separates him from the crowd. Success is not always measured by achievement; sometimes it is simply the ability to see things differently.

Perhaps that is why he is smiling.

COMMENTS:

Jordana has a cute idea and therein is its limitation. Certainly it shows initiative and a coherent style to present her deviant goldfish is such glowing terms. Alas, it also reflects the slick condensation of advertising, replete with audiovisual aids. Is the fish breathing a little too heavily perhaps? (SAB)

I like this. It is simply written but makes a powerful statement for independence that most students (and adults) can relate to. Using the *Goldfish* heading catches the reader's attention. (BPS)

Arielle Simon
College: Wellesley College

The mid-July, New York City smog was just beginning to settle over Manhattan as I approached the brown apartment building on the corner of Bowery and Stanton. Although I had prepared extensively, I was apprehensive, having never given a workshop for eight-year-olds before. However, it was when Joyce, the leader of the group, arrived and changed the topic of the workshop that I panicked.

I work as a peer educator for NARAL/NY (National Abortion and Reproductive Rights Action League, New York Chapter), an organization focused mainly on abortion, reproductive rights and related issues. Though the choice of eight-year-old-friendly topics for which I had been trained was not extensive, I managed to produce a comprehensive workshop on grassroots advocacy for the group of second graders in the ten minutes I was allotted.

After the workshop ended—and it had gone remarkably well—Joyce took me aside to congratulate me and thank me for my work. Then somewhat apologetically, she said, "Don't worry if they weren't completely attentive, they never listen to women." I never expected to hear this remark from the mouth of an educator, particularly a woman, and for a moment I was completely astounded and speechless. There seemed to be a great disparity between the way I had managed to create a seemingly impossible workshop under a time constraint, and the way in which I was viewed based solely upon my gender. It seemed as though it didn't matter how hard I worked or how impressive my work was, I would still, at times, be viewed primarily as a woman. I was frustrated with the notion that things cannot change, that we must accept gender inequalities graciously. I was frustrated that no one was attempting to teach these children, at the very least, to be respectful of others.

I have seen how gender boundaries can be extremely paralyzing and harmful. I have been in classrooms where women who were rarely called on and often preempted by men have stopped speaking and stopped listening. I have seen women, stereotyped by their gender to be passive and dependent, actually grow into these expectations. Throughout my work as a peer educator for NARAL/NY, I have seen the difficulties and rewards in undoing and unteaching stereotypes and misinformation. I became a peer educator because I have seen how gender boundaries can be destructive and I believe that the best remedy has always been, without fail, education.

I left that brown apartment building on the corner of Bowery and Stanton, pondering Joyce's words. Literary critic Stephen Greenblatt has said, "... *we can scarcely write of prince or poet without accepting the fiction that power directly emanates from him [or her] and that society draws upon this power.*" In other words, one cannot be overpowered unless s/he grants power to the authority. Joyce was overpowered. She assumed a powerless position by devaluing women herself.

Throughout my work at NARAL, as an intern at NOW (National Organization for Women, New York City chapter), and as leader of the Gender Issues Committee of the Dalton School, I work to erase the stereotypes that keep women passive and silent on a daily basis. Reflecting on Joyce's words, I learned a tremendous amount about the continuing pervasive power of gender boundaries and how, in subtle and overt ways, women have learned to believe them. I have come to have a renewed appreciation for the individual—one who operates not based on expected roles and stereotypes, not upon the notion of what one should or shouldn't be, but one who is motivated and inspired by personal ideals, ambitions and the desire for true equality for all people. This, I believe, is personal freedom and sovereignty, and it is a quality for which I continuously strive.

COMMENT:

This is an interesting essay because it shows us the writer at work in a number of ways. She is trying to understand something upsetting that happened to her—not solely to narrate it—and to use that experience as a way to think more broadly. In other words, we see a mind at work here. She doesn't know all the answers, nor should she. But as someone who believes in education, she has been startled by a professional educator's apparent collapse under the weight of gender inequalities. This writer feels indignant about the danger of inaction. We get the sense that she'll be an active and engaged college student. (MR)

Ann Cox
College: Harvard University

I could tell you all about my wonderful achievements, slightly exaggerated of course, but I'd rather tell you what affects me, what I remember. The things like the way the six shadows of my tennis racket converged on the ball as it sat clearly marked in its yellow on the huge green court. And how the same ball was caught in the net by the back wall, like a fish. The way the herring plane in Maine swoops down on me all little on the long field. And the piece of hay stuck between my toes that stayed with me even as I went in to talk to my old aunt. How I promised to remember that and the time I was walking down the marble stairs of St. Ann's in my green knit skirt so I would know I existed then, that my past was not something simply planted in my brain. The way I've felt myself growing, almost physically, and listened to my growth settling into me, and welcomed it because it meant I was becoming more realistic about myself, so that not living in a world of illusions I could exist more in this world and feel all its happinesses and wonders which are greater than anything imagined because they are real—the most amazing thing of all.

The things that I love to feel and discover are the subtleties happening between people and events. How one person helplessly tries to make himself known to others, the way the others might ignore him, and the way he will stay with the others as friends because he's been saved from something he doesn't want to acknowledge anyway. The way masses or a nation of people will ignore some huge, very true situation, and then slowly discover it in a way that's as useless as if they'd never found it. The way I myself fit into everyone's patterns and the way my actions affect me, why they make me feel good or bad, and whether they really do. The things that are observed and given: trees, animals, ourselves, snow, and winds. Using my body to certain ends and to an end in itself: sexual, transportation, exploration, and to an immersion into an environment and discovering the physical realities of the world, as skiing does. Traveling, the feeling of "wanderlust" raging and satisfied, going wherever I wish to, encountering, dealing with, and enjoying new people, situations, and places.

And somewhere within this huge scheme of myself, learning fits in as a major part. Education brings all these parts of the world to me, and me to them, and I can work them and myself, as I use my own mind to deal with them, cast light on them, and encompass them. And so now I wish to present myself at one of the "great educational institutions" to gather, process, and give more.

COMMENT:

I liked the unsettling tone of the essay. The opening reminded me of Kenneth Koch's poetry—the images are startling and disconcerting. The essay walks a thin line, though, since it comes close to being so abstract and fuzzy that it loses its impact. The daring, almost free association saves it. I think, though, it's one of the weaker essays in this group. (PT)

Theodore C. Dros
College: Hamilton College

In his movie, *Zelig,* Woody Allen portrays a figure, Zelig, with a multiple personality. He changes his character and even his physical appearance to match the different situations he experiences. One minute he is waving to us from Hitler's entourage during a speech, the next, he is a cardinal in the Vatican, or up at bat for the New York Yankees. All of these experiences in his life are divorced from one another, each exists as an entirely separate entity, having no connection to his past or future. He is, in other words, the perfect chameleon, about whom we are left to wonder, "Who is the real Zelig?"

What I understand you to be asking me to address here is "who is the real Ted Dros?" As I began to answer that difficult question, I find myself needing "to do a Zelig" by relating to you some of the diverse environments in which I've been immersed over the last five or six years.

Growing up in a changing community during the sixth to eighth grades, I saw my grammar school, Our Lady of Refuge in Brooklyn, face a dramatic ethnic shift in enrollment. Over a few short years, the school population changed from being predominantly Caucasian to being almost totally black and Hispanic. I graduated as one of two "minority students" in the class, and I was treated as one. On the one hand, my teachers of my own race alienated me from my classmates by anticipating that I would perform "par excellence." On the other hand, my own desire to be accepted by my fellow students required me to hold back academically—to resist answering all the questions. There were definitely moments when I was tempted to get up and walk out on a system that was insensitive to the needs of someone who didn't conform to the majority, but I didn't. Instead, I withstood all of the unjust treatment that a minority typically has to endure. Having had the shoe on the other foot for that period of my life, however, I now more fully understand the injustice and resultant moral outrage that blacks and Hispanics must experience in our society-at-large.

In striking contrast, summertime has always provided me an opportunity to explore another side of life. During this time my family and I stay at my grandmother's summer beach house in Breezy Point, Queens. Consisting primarily of middle-class Irish families, this community has been a part of my life since birth and has served to put me in touch with my own ethnicity. At Breezy Point there is an

Irish concern with ancestral lineage, a deep-rooted pride in family, and an interest in folk dance and music. My family, as are most in Breezy Point, is closely tied to an active religious life. Perhaps grounded in centuries of Irish oppression, the community is a hot-bed of religious, social, and cultural bonding.

Finally, at the end of the summer four years ago, a totally new and unexplored environment, one that was chiefly academic, was first introduced into my life. At Regis striving for academic excellence was encouraged by all. It was quite a different situation than grammar school. Regis High School propelled me into another world—one that was more white middle- to upper-class and "preppy" than I had ever known. It gave me freedom through which I was able to pursue my interests with confidence, voice my opinions, exercise my right to be wrong, and accomplish my goals. As the result of being accepted for who I really was, I became more at ease with my world.

Given the three vastly different environments that I have just described in this self-descriptive essay, I imagine it's pretty easy for you to understand why I should think of myself as a Zelig-figure. There is, however, a striking difference between us: Zelig—chameleon that he is—totally adapts to his various environments and looks at each one as if it were an isolated set of circumstances. The effect of the diverse environments I have known on my perception has been dramatically different from that on his. I assimilate to the point of being comfortable with retaining my identity. As a matter of fact, when I move on from these learning experiences, I take a part of them with me: an idea, thought, feeling, emotion—a certain understanding.

This carryover from experience helps to explain why I still find it exciting to be teaching parish CCD classes at my old grammar school to Haitian, Jamaican, and Puerto Rican children. It also accounts for the enthusiasm I bring to the summer job I have held for three years at the Silver Gull Beach Club in the Rockaways. Here I cater to another cultural group—a Jewish community—of which I had no prior knowledge, but which I found myself drawn toward as a contrast to my Breezy Point Irish heritage.

While the answer to the question "who is Ted Dros?" may vary at any given moment according to my environment, I have, unlike the schizophrenic Zelig, a single, though evolving personality. While I value multiplicity of situations and diversity among people precisely because they prompt my personal growth, I do at most points know and like who I am. It's just that, building on my past, I also look forward to the person I will be tomorrow.

COMMENTS:

This student completes a difficult task with excellence. His initial analogy to Zelig arouses the reader's attention. He describes his varied experiences in a clear, concise form that flows naturally from one to another. I would have no difficulty accepting him for both his background and his description of it. (TG)

A well-written, clear account of Ted Dros, whom the reader knows quite well after reading it. Where many essay writers may have fallen into a rather tedious autobiographical format . . . "I was born . . . ," Ted has neatly woven Woody Allen's *Zelig* to create a thorough, interesting, and informative essay. (JWM)

Cody Corliss
College: Harvard University

AN APPALACHIAN VIEW

As I reached the top of the country ridge, my jog gradually slowed to a walk. I looked to my right and saw my cross-country teammates gathered together enjoying the picturesque view. I walked over to them.

I gazed out upon the green rolling hills, but my eyes soon fixed upon the tiny community below nestled between the hills and the mighty Ohio River. I knew the town well for it was my hometown, the place where I first learned to ride a bicycle, attended my first day of school, and first learned to drive a car.

A teacher once told me that nearly everything that I would come to believe would be rooted in my hometown. As I looked out upon my home connected to the outside world by a two-lane road, I understood the meaning of those prophetic words. This community has taught and instilled every value that I hold true today. I've learned to value hard work from the laborers who produce power, chemicals, and steel in the nearby plants and mills along the river. My school and community have taught me to value education and to develop a hunger for learning. My grandmother has taught me to be honest and compassionate while my mother has instilled my vision and self-discipline.

More than any other value, I have been taught to be loyal. I know that I will soon have to leave my home to attend college. Yet I am compelled to return to West Virginia. I am compelled to return out of duty and loyalty for this place that I love. West Virginia needs leaders to enhance education and improve an economy plagued with inadequacy since the Civil War. The plants and mills that provide jobs for my community are owned by companies from outside of West Virginia. According to a 1990 Appalachian Regional Commission study, seventy-five percent of the land and eighty percent of the mineral rights are owned by out-of-state interests. Sadly, if West Virginia were a third-world country, we would be called a colony.

Many of my friends talk of leaving West Virginia and never returning. I understand their views, but I disagree. I look forward to the day that I can return and make an impact. We must take back our state. It is time to return to the tradition of the proud mountaineer. This place, formed by Lincoln's pen and forged in the fires of war, will improve only through the combined efforts of all of West Virginia's best and brightest.

I admit that I am excited about the prospect of attending college and meeting new people. I cherish the thought of having the opportunity to meet and interact with people from all different backgrounds and cultures. I await the chance to gain insight from exposure to new ideas and new views. These are the ultimate goals of any college education. I know though that even when I am away from home, I'll always be influenced by West Virginia. I take pride in the fact that my values will always trace back to a tiny community nestled along the banks of the mighty Ohio River and connected to the outside world by a two-lane road.

COMMENT:

This essay has a clear focus and makes a clear point. It tells a good deal about both the writer and the importance of place upon him. The first two paragraphs seem quite vague and dreamy; I was worried. Would the writer ever abandon abstractions and generalities and get down to specifics? Fortunately, he does. He comes from a particular place that has meant something quite particular to him. Loyalty is what he learned in his home state of West Virginia, and loyalty is what he holds himself responsible to return to it. (MR).

Don Hoffman
College: Amherst College

AN ESSAY

I am a product of hippies, he wrote, startled that he had begun with such an idea. It was an interesting way to begin, he pondered, though not totally accurate. He wasn't actually a *product* of hippies, but he had been given a brief, fleeting vision through their eyes. Yes . . . he and Joan Didion had walked through the place where the kissing never stopped, they had met Comrade Laski, they had taken courses at the Joan Baez School; his visions had caused him to rede-fine his beliefs. Was his outlook on his life his own, or had his ideas been passed on to him like genes? He sat outside on the Senior Patio and read her book, *Slouching Towards Bethlehem;* "space is a place" was written on his jeans in the spirit of Hippie Day. He believed he was a product of the ideas he encountered; shouldn't it be that way?

I am a product of everything, really. Just as he wrote, he noticed that he was finally doing it: writing these dreaded essays. He once knew a friend who had visited the Temple of Essays. As he was being lowered down into the pit, he could hear the awful hiss of the essays below him, like snakes. "I hate snakes," he thought, helplessly. What did they want? The meaning of life on paper. He could give them the fundamental theorem of calculus, the definition of Newtonian rela-tivity, perhaps the three qualities of good writing, but only if he re-ferred to his notes from September.

He had a great idea for an essay, but it passed like a gray freight train on the tracks near the river, where trains were no longer that frequent. Another idea came, then a multitude of others, pouring down on the paper as if falling from the waterfall in North Carolina named Silver Run. Some were tears, perhaps, bits of the soul. When he looked at the paper, he saw that the ideas had soaked it and made it soggy and impossible to read.

Then, there was a knock at the door. He opened it with trepida-tion, fearing a younger brother or perhaps another terror not so bad as that. Standing there was an original idea for an essay, naked and somewhat unformed. He wrestled with it, questioning it until he became a part of it. His life was merely an extension of this wonder-ful yet terrible idea, swirling like a hurricane. In his humanities class at school he was studying World War I, but he often felt like *he* was the one in the trenches. He was called daily to charge some great unseen idea. He used his pen as the sword, often finding it an unsuit-able weapon. He never knew who won his war, but he knew by his grades that he had won at least a few important battles.

Besides fighting ideas, he was fighting to establish himself. He was fighting against being seen as impersonal; he was fighting against impersonal things. He loved dwelling on his own personal ideas, experiences, emotions. He had fought a grand battle with standardized tests. Could it be that this one important battle would change his life?

I don't think standardized tests deal with ideas, he realized. He *did* have aptitudes, but one for lapsing into extremes. But he enjoyed this because he often learned more because of it. Whether he explored Brighton or Bethlehem, he did so with both joy and fear. He loved ideas as well, writing English papers when the ideas flowed freely from him. Then, he actually believed in what he wrote, hearing the words, like foreign voices. He realized that ideas were not the only things that could possess him. Music controlled him too, signing him up for the church and school choirs, making him audition for musicals, driving him to create songs on the piano.

Other things control me too, he continued. He loved running, but often felt that he temporarily relinquished control of himself when he ran, as when he wrote English papers. When he ran, he sometimes felt that he would not be able to finish the race, he would have to stop and rest. He often wondered why he ran, as it was so difficult. The words of the coach, however, had given him a vision, an idea, to commit himself to the run: As the run came to an end, he always felt refreshed. He would be ready for tomorrow, he promised, he would get out there and run hard again, challenge himself, sometimes not knowing why but running hard just the same.

I am controlled by what I do, he rewrote.

COMMENT:

The author is controlled by metaphors and similes rather than having control over them. The ideas are complex and the writer is clearly intelligent. But, as he tries to show his complexity as a person, he loses control of the essay. The result is diminished by overabundance. (PLF)

Josh Jacobs
College: Amherst College

Some people, I am quite sure, go through all of high school without a single moment of social hesitance or exclusion. I would imagine that many cheerleaders and football players fit this mold—at least, that's what I've always heard. At any rate, I certainly have not had a maintenance-free high school social life; however, aside from the Whipped-Puppy Crush, which most adolescent males suffer at least once, I have had only one major watershed in these four years, a time when I realized that the past was ending, and that the future could go anywhere. This was when my best friend of four years, who I will refer to as The Philistine (or TP, for short), totally severed relations with me in the first weeks of my junior year.

An unsigned *New Yorker* editorial once described a true crisis as one in which ". . . for a measurable, anguished period . . . nothing happens. Truly nothing. . . . At a false turning point, we nearly always know, within limits, what will happen next; at a true turning point, we not only know nothing, but know that nobody knows. Truly nobody." As in this quote, I had several weeks in which I had no idea what to do. I had always been aware of the fact that TP was better-looking than I, and more confident as well. The fact that TP picked up a steady girlfriend midway through my time in Coventry brought me to the conclusion that I had become too great a burden on him, that my function as an amusing second banana had ended. I was becoming aware of the fact that there had always been a certain coolness about TP, one which I had not been exposed to being his friend. At times, I thought TP would come to me and apologize, and that all would be sweetness and light once more; I came to realize, however, that I could never accept such an apology in the unlikely event that it were to be proffered. Once revealed, a person's true feelings are nearly impossible to plow under again.

It was during this bitter time that I first became friendly with my current group of closest friends. I believe that I was attracted to them because, not to demean their maturity or complexity, I sensed that there was something about them that was more willing to care, and much less cynical and begrudging than TP was. It was hard to say why they were attracted to me; I do not remember trying particularly hard to impress them with my wit or intelligence, perhaps because I did not realize completely that I was growing closer to these people. It may be that my subconscious mind was, in a subliminal way, going all-out, realizing that this was a golden opportunity to make a transition from knowing and trusting just one person to having several confidantes.

It is with this group that I have spent the happiest months of my life. To be loved is the most joyful, most uplifting emotional state; giving of one's own love is a close second place, however, and with these friends I have had both. I have become more outgoing and spontaneous, and quite a bit sillier—in short, I feel better about being myself. Reflecting on the friendship that TP and I once had, I can say that the saddest lesson that I learned from my transitory semester in high school is that the best things in life are often the hardest to preserve, the hardest to hold on to; in the words of Robert Frost, "Nothing gold can stay."

COMMENTS:

My concern is that the essay appears to tell more about "TP" than about Josh Jacobs! I think that the topic of rejection is an interesting one. However, it would have been far better for me to know *specifically* how "JJ" has ". . . become more outgoing and spontaneous . . . sillier." The final paragraph is weakened by the use of generalizations. While candid about his relationships, Josh may be too confident about what he perceives as the reasons for the demise of his friendship. (AAF)

In my opinion, this is a very good essay. The organization and sentence structure are first-rate, the vocabulary provocative and appropriate, and the literary allusions are apt and unobtrusive. The writer gives us a lot of insight into the kind of person he is without making himself seem unduly boastful. It is an effective bit of writing. (RCM)

Joseph Libson
College: Princeton University

My Life

Chapter One: I become a truant

The best thing that I ever did for myself was skip nine days of school in a row in the eighth grade. Actually the benedictions did not arise so much from the truancy as from the apprehension. This does not mean that I had been an axe murderer for the previous sections of my life, but rather that an unusual circumstance led to a great improvement in almost every aspect of my life. I was getting mediocre grades (i.e., B's and C's) at a mediocre school. I was not taking drugs or doing anything particularly nasty, but I was being incredibly lazy. This sudden burst of lethargy that led to the nine-day truancy overcame the activation barrier that had prevented my parents from taking retaliatory measures in response to all of the smaller things that I had done. Their response was draconian; first they separated me and my brother (we are exponentially more troublesome when together). In addition to deciding to send me to another school to separate me and my brother, my parents also decided that the punishment should extend into the summer since the deed had been done late in April and the school's punishment of nine Saturday detentions (yes, like the ones in *The Breakfast Club*) and disciplinary probation seemed insufficient. This planting season sentence consisted of my taking summer courses. Thus, it came to pass that I took algebra II before ninth grade.

When I arrived at Walnut Hills, which is the best academic public school in the city, I knew no one. This temporary exile resulted in a great discovery. Since I had no one to talk to during class, I decided that I would listen to see if the teacher was saying anything interesting. Lo and behold, knowledge flowed into and through me as excellent grades flowed out. At the tender age of thirteen, I had discovered that if I listened, I would understand. I had four straight-A quarters at Walnut Hills and transferred to St. Xavier, an even finer institution. It was closer to home and besides that my parents had heard that it was a "tough" no-nonsense school (good for discipline problems). As an additional plus, due to variances between the curricula of Walnut Hills and St. Xavier, I was able to become two years advanced in mathematics. Thus I was taking BC Calculus during my junior year at St. Xavier. My innovative listening theory still held at St. Xavier although more effort had to be put in to get the same grades simply because St. Xavier was a more difficult school.

Skipping nine days of school made me a better person, there is no doubt about it. Not only did my academics improve, but my devotion to athletics was enhanced to that of a religious fanatic and my sense of morals was even improved. I changed from a selfish rather unfriendly and sarcastic person into a more giving and open (but still sarcastic) individual. But, I was lucky; I got caught.

COMMENT:

The truant manages to show the reader, in very few words, just how much perspective he has on his past experiences. His focus on "getting caught" highlights his obvious self-awareness because it is so "unadolescent" of him to see his "getting caught" and being "punished" as a catalyst to his own intellectual and personal growth of which he is so clearly proud. This anecdote had a strong impact on me because it rings true and because Joe's tone is very sincere. (AST)

Heather L. Nadelman
College: Yale University

"Coffee or tea?"

A simple enough question, a question that seemingly requires an absentminded, automatic reply. Clearly, in this world one is either a coffee or a tea drinker. I, however, am an exception to this rule; I constantly vacillate between coffee and tea. My enjoyment of both drinks does not stem merely from flexible tastebuds, nor does it originate in a desire to be as little trouble as possible by drinking whatever is available. Rather, this ambivalence depicts two distinct sides of my personality.

Coffee is lively, exuberant, and extroverted: a wild, wet dog show, complete with pouring rain, whipping winds, and a dog who simply will not behave. The ring has become a sea of oozing mud, turning the dog you so perfectly groomed last night into a mud-splattered, bedraggled horror who resembles an alley cat more than a purebred show dog with a pedigree going back to the *Mayflower*. Animals who never before had shown signs of unstable temperament suddenly decide to be terrified of the wind's flapping their handlers' yellow rain slickers. All dogs are quick to take advantage of the fact that their handlers, with fingers numbed from cold and eyes half-blinded from rain, have very little control over them. On such a day, a steaming cup of well-brewed hot coffee is one's only salvation; only coffee can transform such misery into a memory that will be laughably, almost fondly, recalled.

Tea is sedate, thoughtful, and introverted: a cold November afternoon with a friendly fire crackling in the background. One sits in an overstuffed armchair with an open copy of *Wuthering Heights*, reading, dreaming, and listening to music that plays softly from the stereo. The novel and music flow into each other, transporting the room to a time that perhaps was, perhaps never was, or perhaps always is. The world's worries are locked outside, flung to the chilly winds; inside, all is peaceful and relaxed. On such an afternoon, one feels able to solve every riddle that the greatest minds have pondered. Yet oddly, on such afternoons one never attempts solutions. So near the point of understanding, one allows all answers to escape; if the mysteries of life were solved, much of the pure pleasure of thinking would be lost forever. At such moments of partial meditation it is tea, the world's most civilized drink, that is one's only conceivable companion.

Although often contradictory, my need for coffee and my need for tea balance each other nicely. The freneticism of the world of dog shows is as important as the quiet reflection of a peaceful afternoon. Perhaps I will originate a new personality classification, the "coffeetean," roughly equivalent to an introverted-extrovert or extroverted-introvert. Unlike the simple lives of people wholly shy or wholly exuberant, the life of a coffeetean, if a bit complicated, cannot fail to be varied and exciting.

Those who drink coffee, tea, and hot chocolate, however, are far too schizophrenic for their own good.

COMMENTS:

An interesting, relatively original, although somewhat contrived way of presenting two sides of her personality. The purpose of the essay is a good one—to attempt to give a clearer picture of how she sees herself. (JWM)

A rather abstract evaluation of a very simple idea. The vocabulary appears to be forced at times, possibly in an attempt to impress the reader. The well-chosen analogies, however, reveal a very imaginative student who expresses her ideas with both brevity and clarity. (TG)

Travis Hallett
College: Harvard University

LIKE COOTIES

They were unable to hide the fact that they were all looking at me. Some wore expressions of disgust, but I took mental note of the few who seemed to understand. Even the teachers were obvious. Those who knew me stared and the ones who had only heard the rumors nervously looked away. I kept trying to make my way to chemistry so that I could be on time for once, and I watched the other students part around me like the Red Sea. I wasn't anything close to Moses—I wasn't even any different than the days or even years before. But everything was different now, without as much as a single change.

It's not like my closest friends and I haven't known I was gay since the dawn of time. I mean, I was *in love* with a guy I barely knew when I was in second grade. And please, my iTunes playlists really don't make it difficult to tell that I'm gay. When people ask, I tell them the truth. I just assume that everyone else knows. I would never describe myself as a walking stereotype, but usually those who are less than completely naïve can figure it out. So it came as a big surprise to me when I found out that most people who go to my school didn't know I was gay. The way that *they* found out, though, makes my surprise seem trivial.

There was this guy. Of course, I was completely infatuated with him. But as all seemingly sad stories go there's a horrible twist. Rick had been a good friend of mine for as long as my memory holds. He's into girls. More specifically, one of my best friends, Sarah. The details were furiously text-messaged. The drama that ensued was honestly worthy of bad daytime television. In his complete obliviousness, Rick didn't figure it out when everyone else did. With some friends rooting me on or pushing me into a pit (I couldn't tell), I decided to confront him.

It was hard to find time to actually talk to Rick about it what with his grandmother dying and senior week activities. We finally did get a chance to talk one night, after he was finished working, in the Burger King parking lot. I was leaning against my dusty grey car trying to calculate the correlation between Rick's feelings and how far away he stood. Minutes went by between exchanges of words as I kept searching for the right ones, but to no avail. The omnipresent Maine mosquitoes were swarming the two of us and the flickering parking lot lamp above. All of my internal organs did a few somersaults when he told me how he felt. I had expected him to never want anything to do with me again, but he was okay with my crush. It obviously needed to end for us to have some sort of working relationship, but it was nothing like I had feared. Thank God. When it was all said and done I asked him if we were cool, and as he was walking out to the bus to go on project grad minutes after graduation a few days later, we hugged and then fist bumped. All was well.

When I left my high school after that day with one year still left to go, I felt relieved. After weeks of yelling and then spans of suspenseful silence with all of my friends involved in this one-sided love scandal, everyone's now-tested acceptance was much appreciated. As I did my speed walk through the Red Sea and all the way to room 118 after the word had gotten out nearly as fast as the speed of light, I knew I was lucky to have such accepting friends. I know for sure now that I don't need to hide anything around them. It has allowed me to be more like myself around more people than ever. With being gay, there's definitely a difference between people saying they're fine with it and their actually being fine with it. I knew I would lose friends in the process. Caribou High's tolerance was pushed to its breaking point and a few people are now missing from my friends list on Facebook. It's for the best, though, because I would definitely rather sacrifice some "friends" for my freedom to be me. In a school marred by the intolerance that our civil rights team has tried to combat, I'm now glad to be liberated, being outed to everyone who didn't know, because no matter if it's because I'm Moses or because everyone is afraid to catch my gay germs, I'm proud to be the one who now parts the sea.

COMMENT:

I liked this kid. From the moment I started to read I heard his voice in my head, and I wanted to know why everyone was looking at him. He opened with a great hook, continued the story to the conclusion. This student wasn't looking to be a trailblazer for the community. In fact he rather mundanely detailed a pivotal aspect of his life with subtle bravery. The writer is specific and connects with the reader. Could I see him in a freshman English class at Harvard? I cannot tell from simply this essay; however, I do envision whatever college campus he lands upon will be lucky to have him. Kudos, kid. (BLB)

Phillip Rodgers
College: Columbia College

Demosthenes, Moses, Winston Churchill, and Somerset Maugham. You're probably wondering what possible link these great men of years past could have to this piece about Phil Rodgers. Furthermore, you're probably thinking that they have no apparent relation to each other. One was an orator, one a biblical figure, one a statesman, and still another an author. But a little-known fact is that all of these men were stutterers. Add me to the list.

To fulfill your clinical curiosity, I'm classified as a secondary stutterer, which means that I was not born with the malady. At age eight, for some not yet diagnosed reason, I simply began speaking dysfluently. A quick mathematical operation tells one that I've been stuttering for nine years. My family seems to prefer to think of it as that I was fluent for eight.

But sometimes I wish that I didn't have the memories of my period of fluent speech. My mother, whom I love dearly and upon whom I place no blame for my problem, always speaks of me when the subject of children arises. She talks of how bright and intelligent I was, and how I loved to talk and be inquisitive. My big claim to fame was my relative eloquence at an early age. This is why I sometimes wish that I had been born a stutterer. My relatives, my parents, and most importantly, I, know what it was like for me to speak fluently. This knowledge imposes a feeling of guilt along with the other negative feelings associated with my speech problem. Guilt for not giving my parents the perfect son. Guilt for not being what I could have been. Guilt for not being a whole person.

But the guilt is only part of it. The more dominant feeling is frustration. Frustration perhaps about what I'm not to my family, but more importantly about what I'm not to myself. I want nothing more in this world than to make my family, and myself, proud of me. I want to make a contribution to somebody or something that will make a difference. But when the situation is such that I encounter an opportunity to make a contribution that may be hindered by my stuttering, my initial response is to shy away. And if the hindrance will burden others, I back off completely. As far as I see it, the problem is mine and I have no right to impose upon others to any greater extent than that which is necessary in verbal communication. As a result, I don't experience all that life has to offer. Frustration.

This is not to say that I've withdrawn from society. I truly believe the old maxim that whatever can be conceived and believed can be achieved. And if I attain nothing else in my life, this is what I want to do. Perhaps this sounds like a rather trivial goal, but what I desire most is to be fluent. I want nothing more than to express my feelings, thoughts, opinions without the ugliness of my stuttering in the foreground. But if I can't make my contribution to the world fluently, then I'll have to do it as I am.

However, contributing can get painful. Every time I open my mouth I take the risk of being jeered, laughed at, labelled "retarded," and so forth. And the hurt that I've experienced has stayed with me. All of the jokes, the insults, and the feelings of inferiority rarely expressed remain in my memory as clearly as yesterday. And I'm glad they do. They give me the strength to cope with what to me is a serious shortcoming. When I'm up against a situation in which I might be vulnerable, all I need do is recall the pain and almost desperate loneliness, and somehow I draw strength from it. The strength that I need to achieve all that I want to achieve. The strength to survive.

I recall a drawing I did in sixth grade. I composed it after being physically and emotionally humiliated in a brawl by three older boys who said that they didn't want a "retard" in their school. The drawing was a tear-stained image of a butterfly in a cage. That's a metaphor for who I am. I am a person wanting to share so much with the world, but encircled by a barrier stronger than that of any steel. I am a person wanting to express every thought, every emotion, but stymied by a force that is out of my realm of control. I am a person wanting to be able to speak without fear of ridicule or ostracization, but restrained by a weight greater than that of any physical burden. I am a person wanting to be freed from a perennial hindrance. I am a butterfly who has broken through his socio-erected limitations, but not his own intrinsic weakness.

COMMENT:

My reaction to this essay is one of sympathy for the writer, as much for what he appears to have endured from his family's reaction to his stuttering as for the suffering he has endured as a result of the stuttering itself. His latent handicap seems to have all but engulfed his consciousness to the point where everything in his life is measured in terms of what he cannot do, rather than what he can do. I found myself wanting to say, "It's not your fault *AND* I really don't hold it against you." Somehow I don't think saying anything would help. (AST)

Sara G. Silver
College: Columbia University

It was a beautiful day and my mindcleaning was proceeding nicely. I generally despise any sort of cleaning and avoid it whenever possible, but mindcleaning is different; it's much too important and delicate a job to delay. And it was doubly important that day, for I was debating starting my life anew in New York and I needed to rid my mind of old prejudices to make room for fresh ideas. So I ascended the stairs armed with garbage bag and duster, opened the door to my mind, and went in. Now, everyone has their own particular taste and everyone arranges their mind differently. In mine, all the rooms are arranged on different levels according to category around a big winding staircase done in red velvet plush, and it was to the first level of this staircase that I was ascending on that bright, clear day. Everything on the first level is memories of some type. They are easy to clean because there is nothing to throw away. True, I sometimes push a bad one behind the shelf or sweep it under the rug, but most memories take root too deeply and quickly to be disposed of, although I do misplace quite a few small ones between cleanings. So I just dusted them all off, arranged them neatly in rows, and proceeded onward. On my way up I wrote a reminder to myself to add on a new wing, as the existing rooms were becoming quite crowded, and if there is one thing I can't stand in a room, it's clutter.

The second level is for talents and impulses. Many people think that these are things which come spontaneously and therefore just let them wander freely, but I find it much easier to have them categorized. For instance, how many times have you missed a train because the impulse that should have warned you to arrive at the station earlier was nowhere to be found? And if someone should ask you to show off your singing talent, what if that talent is hiding in a corner and refuses to reveal itself? That's why I categorize mine. Upon going through them, I found a misplaced unfinished thought and carried it up to the third level with me.

The third level is a bit different. It has only two rooms: Miscellaneous, and the Day Room. After I placed the thought safely in Miscellaneous, it was the latter room to which I turned my attention. The Day Room is where all the daily traffic collects to be sorted out each night: with whom I met that day, what each person said, and everything else that transpires. After having attended to this daily task, I sent everything to where it is supposed to be stored via a special elevator I had installed for the purpose and, hopping a ride myself, arrived at the fifth floor. On this level I don't dare to enter the rooms unless there is a pressing emergency, but just peek through the little glass windows to ascertain the working level, for here is the crux of my brainpower—the delicate processing and reasoning machines. I possess only the latest models but I am a terrible novice around such machinery. So with resolutions to gain more experience and then tinker, I just checked a readout or two and went on.

The last level, my favorite, is my knowledge level but I prefer to call it my library. This is also a most important level, although not quite as delicate as the logic machines below. Here, every little thing I learn is recorded and kept safe. After dusting all the shelves, I leafed briefly through a few of the latest volumes to be sure that yesterday's history lectures had been duly recorded. I then hefted my garbage bag under one arm, my duster under the other, and started back down. But as I turned to leave, a door at one end of the library caught my eye. Strangely, I'd never seen it before. I put down my bundle and strode forward to take a closer look. As I opened the deceptively shabby door, a burst of light and color streamed out! Curiously I entered the room—and stopped short, unable to believe my eyes. For beyond the dusky, stately, library lay a wonderful room, a room filled with hope and joy of every color, with sunshine playing gaily over it all. Across the gleaming floorboards I spotted an evanescent figure dressed in red, gold, and white sequins beckoning to me and sparkling until I was nearly blinded. But before I could recover from my surprise enough to wave back, the entire room disappeared and I was left standing in the shadowy library once more.

Bewildered, I picked up my load and descended the stairs, still deep in thought as I left my mind and shut the last door, my task completed. I was filled with a deep fierce longing, for in the one glimpse into that room I had felt more love and color than I had ever dreamed existed within me, and I knew the room's contents were the reason. From then on, I yearned for another glimpse of what I could become. Not until my plane was circling over New York City in the ever-deepening sunset and the city's lights began to twinkle on did I fully understand what that one secret room contained. And it was with hope and relief blossoming anew that I opened the room forever, a small secret smile lingering on my lips.

COMMENTS:

An interesting idea for a personal, revealing essay. It starts off slowly, and seems too "cute" to be effective, but the ending saves it and leaves the reader with an overall impression of a successful piece of writing. (HDT)

This is a wonderful essay with a few basic grammatical flaws. The progression is clear, and the imagination wonderful. (PLF)

Dawn N. Skwersky
College: Mount Holyoke

TELL US ABOUT YOURSELF

Q: What is so great about being deaf?
A: Hey, I can't believe someone finally asked me that! Ok, here's a list:

—If someone is singing off key I can turn them off with a switch.
—Airplanes aren't so loud.

—In the morning when my dog wakes everyone up with his bark-
ing—I stay asleep.

—People can yell in my ears.

—Music sounds great without my aids because I have low frequency
hearing, which is what most music is.

—Nothing is too loud. If, in a rare instant, something is too loud, I
can switch the noise off.

—I learned to read lips; I usually have face-to-face contact with
people when I talk.

—I developed a predilection for watching subtitled movies and
close-captioned TV shows.

—I am a lifer at a school for the hearing.

—Um . . .

Q: WHOA! A school for the HEARING? How did you end up there?
A: My parents placed me in the school. The funny thing is that I
never thought I was any different. My parents raised me as if I were
a hearing kid.

Q: Wasn't it tough?
A: Yeah, especially when I got older, the guys think I like them because I'm always looking at them, but that's how I read lips.

Q: Hey, but that's still a good excuse to use to stare at guys anyway.
A: Yeah.

Q: How did you take notes in class?
A: That was tough, but I was able to handle that. You see, my success in taking notes depended on

a) my lip reading skills
b) the professor's voice and enunciation skills
c) my position in the classroom
d) all of the above

However, if the teacher was too hard for me to understand (enun-
ciatively) then usually a friend of mine took notes for me.

Q: Did you take any foreign languages?

A: Why do you ask?

Q: I was wondering if you could lip read in other languages.

A: As a matter of fact, I've taken French for five years. In the third year the classes were conducted *tout en français*. It was hard at first, but I was able to adapt to this situation. I guess I have a gift in lip reading languages.

Q: That's awesome. What is bad about being deaf?

A:—Phone conversations are difficult. Not too many people have TTY's (Teletypewriters) or TDD's (Telecommunications Device for the Deaf).

—I can't hear everything around me. For example, it is hard for me to keep up with everything that is said in a social discussion, unless I can see everyone so I can lip read what is being said.

—People usually need to repeat things for me.

—I hate to do the dishes.

Q: Wait a moment! Dishes are irrelevant!

A: That's true, but I said that because doing the dishes bugs me and there is one thing that really bugs me about being deaf.

Q: What is that?

A: I don't like it when people turn their backs to me because they think I may be dull or because they hate repetitions. How can a person judge me who doesn't know me? As for repetitions, the more I talk to a person the fewer repetitions there are. In any case, I've learned through experience that those people who don't take their time when they talk to me aren't true friends.

Q: One last question, is there anything you really want to do in life that you just can't keep secret any longer?

A: Yes, there is.

Q: Ok! let me hear—no, on the other hand, let me lip read it!

A: I WANT TO SPEND MY COLLEGE YEARS AT MOUNT HOLYOKE!

COMMENT:

Let's forgive the ending. It shows a nice sense of humor and much maturity and self-awareness. The writer exhibits good control. (JMcC)

Julia Marie Smith
College: Bowdoin College

'Orphan' best describes my outward appearance at the beginning of my ninth-grade year at Annie Wright. My plain white blouse was more frequently than not untucked; my Campbell plaid skirt hung randomly from nonexistent hips; and my yellow class-tie, which kept unknotting by itself, gave my face a distinctly hepatitic cast. To complete the picture of a lost child, my navy blue socks resisted all efforts to remain below my knees, preferring to bunch down over scrawny ankle bones. This was Julia Smith, new student, adrift in the awful experience of her first school uniform. Not only did I learn to manage my uniform as I grew into it and myself, but I found that this seemingly dreadful mandatory outfit was to become a catalyst for individuality, mine and that of my fellow students. Just as in science sulfuric acid brings about the conversion of butane to isobutane, a school uniform stimulates the development of a set of characteristics which make a specific person unique among others without contributing to that uniqueness. Because everyone looks alike on the outside, uniforms force the emergence of distinct inner qualities. Individuality, thus, cannot be and is not expressed by a superficial style of dress; people at Annie Wright become themselves just because they don't have to, and because they don't want to reflect the mundane nature of our required attire.

I have worn my Campbell plaid skirt for four years and its effect on me will remain with me for the rest of my life. My uniform has caused me to grow into myself as I grew into it, and has caused me to discover my quirks, my druthers, my strengths, and my weaknesses. I am a perfectionist, and yet, if I had those druthers, I would rather spend a lot of time outside enjoying nature or reading a book. I have great determination and perseverance, and yet I am still shy in new situations.

As one member of a school which includes some three hundred students dressed alike according to size, I can attest to my independence from the mob. I have learned to look beyond the uniform in others, eager to search out their special qualities. Pleated polyester in blue and green has enabled me to ignore the outward and superficial appearances of people and has allowed me to treasure their differences. The students at Annie Wright may look like lemmings, but they do not behave like them.

My uniform now fits me, and I no longer look like a neglected orphan. My skin has gradually accustomed itself to the color yellow; the hours spent ironing the rumples the washing machine inflicted on countless pleats and my struggles with recalcitrant socks have been worthwhile. I have accepted my uniform as I have grown beyond the need for a catalyst for individuality. I am Julia Smith, a distinct person, about to begin the next stage of my life adventures.

COMMENT:

The first paragraph is interesting, but the topic doesn't milk well. The essay is cliché-ridden. (JMcC)

Dimitri Steinberg
College: Princeton University

"It is a truth universally acknowledged" that things which come hardest taste sweetest and thus make all the difference. At the beginning of tenth grade, I was, in all honesty, a porker: not obese, perhaps, but definitely overweight. I was also not as popular as I would have wished. I doubt that there was a direct correlation, but I'm sure that my self-esteem was affected by this weighty problem. Although I knew that one's essential substance is more important than superficial show, I could not deny that I was showing more substance, physically, than was desirable. I had carried this burden, on shoulders and hips, since I was eight. In short, at eight, I ate. After several fruitless (but cake-filled) attempts at dieting, I found myself thirty pounds on the wrong side of 140 at age fifteen. I still vividly recall my sincere desire to lose weight, my great love of food, and my frustration.

I needed an incentive to diet. As many previous attempts to shed pounds had gone awry (along with pastrami), a diet seemed a doomed and discredited project. Nevertheless, my parents wisely proposed that all three of us go on a diet and by four weeks the one who had lost the most would be paid $10.00 per pound for each pound the others failed to match. I accepted the challenge. A fierce battle of weights ensued. My chief weapon in this struggle was the 250 callorie Dannon Light strawberry yoghurt. That, and a glass of orange juice was all I consumed until dinner each day. The three S's became my deadliest enemies: starch, snacks and seconds were banished from sight and stomach. The possibility of financial renumeration on one hand or monetary loss on the other overcame my urge to rush the refrigerator. At the weigh-in four weeks later, the scale shoed me minus 13, my mother minus 5, and my father minus 8. I thus extracted a poundage of $130.00 and at the end of the contest I felt as if a huge weight had been shifted from my shoulders to my wallet. What happened afterwards was even more palatable. I had so conditioned my appetite to a glass of orange juice, a cup of yoghurt, and a small dinner that I maintained those eating habits for the rest of the year and thus continued to lose weight until I tipped in at a truly healthy number. I felt better about myself during the second, stabilized phase because I was deriving my pleasure from results gained without ploys or programs.

Before this success, I had often felt myself to be an outsider, looking enviably upon one clique or another. This situation changed quite dramatically. Over the next two years I made many new friends. Just as importantly, I stopped viewing those who weren't my real friends as somehow unapproachable. The inner clique that exists in all high schools and which most everyone aspires to be part of now seemed unappetizing because, having made my own friends, I no longer craved to sit at their table. Losing weight and keeping it off was an accomplishment that allowed me to feel more self-confident. As a result, I was better able to deal with my peers. I got more out of the last two years in and out of school than from all the ones before. The ability to have the discipline to overcome this obstacle has meant a lot to me, not only because of the immediate benefits, but also because of the evidence it gave me about my internal fortitude.

COMMENTS:

This essay shows an excellent writing skill and a good analysis of a marvelous undertaking with positive results to the body and psyche. However, its introspective content suggests a selfish person. (PLF)

Content/idea for the essay is a good one—misspellings detract from it as do all the cute puns—better to stick to the facts and simply tell the tale. The merit lies in the truth, not in the style. (HDT)

Jo-Ellen Truelove
College: Columbia College

From somewhere deep inside the earth's surface, analogies are produced. They seep through the molten lava and the rocks and the soil. They leak into the air and are spirited about like autumn leaves. Eventually, they are seized by English teachers, or solitary philosophers, or those persons who write the verbal section of the SAT, or by people like me: college applicants who, by the light of a fluorescent lamp, hope to structure a profound essay on a comparison. One such analogy has settled upon my own desk, just between the Diet Pepsi can and my lint brush.

I am malleable. I have a tendency to adopt the ideas of others. My philosophy varies with every new author that I read. When I emerged from the theater after seeing *Chariots of Fire,* I was determined to become a sprinter, and ran down the sidewalk in slow motion. After I read Sherlock Holmes, I began studying people while I rode the subway. I tried to uncover bits of their lives by studying their shirt sleeves.

However, like a blob of Play-Doh, I always return to my can with the air-tight lid. Once I ease back into my natural cylindrical shape, I experience my own bursts of creativity. From one such spurt came forth my plan to keep pies fresh in diners. [I believe that if the rotating dessert cases in diners were spun at the speed of light, the pies inside would (in accordance with the Theory of Relativity) actually grow younger as the patrons outside aged normally.] But once I encounter a fresh perspective, I am molded once more.

There are certainly advantages to having an easily sculpted mind. Concepts are more readily understood when they are fully embraced and analyzed. I am also more receptive to new ideas and experiences than many people. In fact, the only real disadvantage is the lack of strong core of self-consciousness. I do not want to go through life with my self-definition being a hodge-podge of outside influences. What to do?

Will Jo-Ellen forever be an impressionable lump? To answer this question, please permit me to stretch my analogy a bit further. When one shapes a Play-Doh masterpiece (a breathtaking likeness of Carmen Miranda, for example) one leaves it on one's bedpost to become more permanent. One might add another fruit to Carmen's hat now and again, but basically, it is set.

At Columbia, I hope to shape myself into a masterpiece that will transcend my humble Play-Doh origins. I want to take advantage of all that the classes, faculty, students, and the City have to offer. Using the insights that I will have collected, my own interpretation of a variety of views, the whole of what I will have gathered from the humanities, and all that I have lived, I will shape myself. And there I will sit proudly on my bedpost—a masterpiece created by the joint efforts of Jo-Ellen Truelove and Columbia College.

In conclusion, I would like to note that some dissimilarities do exist between myself and a can of Play-Doh. So saying, I release my analogy. I send it off, so that it may be used again, to the Analogy Recycling Plant (located in a brownstone just outside of Jersey City).

COMMENTS:

This essay teeters back and forth between being cleverly outrageous and self-consciously cute. Unfortunately, it seems to me that the final paragraph falls into the latter category. There are, on the other hand, some original concepts that are fresh and informative—for instance, the idea for keeping pies fresh in diners and the notion of sticking Carmen Miranda on the bedpost. Technically, the writing is fine. Furthermore, reading the essay gives a clear idea of how the writer views herself in some very important regards. So, on balance, it is a fairly good effort; I just wish she had stopped one paragraph sooner. (RCM)

Shows creativity, imagination, ability. She skillfully carries through her comparison in an engaging lighthearted fashion. I enjoyed it, along with her flashes of humor. Weakness? I thought the essay was a trifle self-conscious—a "quality" she says she lacks. (AAF)

David C. Weymouth
College: University of North Carolina–Chapel Hill

Four-thirty A.M. and the sun was just a sliver of golden promise far to the East. As that sun rose, I began the first day of my summer job. In the fall I would start my first year at St. Paul's, but it was during that summer that I was able to undergo some great changes as a human being. To start with, I was entering the world of lobstering, Maine's oldest and most famous industry. I soon learned there was much more to lobster and lobstering than melted butter and brightly painted buoys. I was aboard a boat ten to twelve hours a day, six days a week, and the work was really hard. This was one thing I learned.

"Sternman" was my official title, a designation which enabled me to do most of the work while the captain (also the owner) would navigate his boat from buoy to buoy. Aside from a ten-minute lunch break, we worked nonstop hauling traps aboard, emptying them of their catch, baiting them, and finally, resetting them. The meaning of "exhaustion" was one more lesson of the summer.

Still, it was not the physical labor that provoked the major change in me. I liked physical labor and was proud of my ability to accomplish so much of it. Rather, it was my introduction to my fellow workers that changed me. Many, if not most of these people, lacked high school diplomas. Surely none had, or would ever receive, a diploma like the one I will earn in June. This is what I discovered that summer; this is what I hauled up in my own personal, metaphorical, lobster trap—the joy of meeting people who, for me, had never before existed.

It was a good joy to experience, and it was a good experience with which to start St. Paul's School. Already, I was coming to St. Paul's much changed from the person who had applied for admission the year before.

Prior to my arrival on the grounds I had been somewhat one-dimensional. Athletically, I was a hockey player, and a hockey player only. I had played other sports, but only rarely and halfheartedly, and only because ice was not available year round. When I came to St. Paul's, I couldn't go out for hockey in the fall. Consequently, I went out for cross-country, figuring, of course, that all the running made it the best sport with which to get in shape for the hockey season. The track on which the cross-country team ran encircled the gridiron, and after several days of running around . . . and around . . . and around it, longingly watching the football practices, I decided I would go out for a different sport and see if my hockey experiences would help me in getting on a football uniform. Since I had never played the game before, getting into my pads was only the first of many lessons I had to learn.

Because the team already had an excess of running backs, or perhaps the coach had seen me running daily on the track and not been as impressed with my speed as I was, I became a lineman. At that time I weighed only 160 pounds, and I can best and with least embarrassment describe the first couple of weeks as . . . "The Time I Learned to Protect My Body." I found myself going up against a defensive lineman referred to only as Hambone. He had slimmed down to a mere 220 pounds over the summer, he rarely shaved, often drooled, and never spoke. Needless to say I picked myself up off my backside more than once during those first few weeks. But I did improve. That year, I played junior varsity. Last year I started on the varsity and was elected to the Second All-League Team. This year I was co-captain of the team and was elected to the First All-League Team.

I still play hockey, and love it, too. But I no longer feel one-dimensional as an athlete.

Academically, I have also arrived at St. Paul's somewhat one-dimensional. I had taken a very ordinary program of math, science, English, and Spanish as my foreign language. Upon coming to St. Paul's, and inspired, perhaps, by too much lobster, I was temporarily insane and dropped Spanish in favor of taking Chinese, which was being offered for the first time.

I must admit that, especially at the beginning, the language was very difficult for me. It was completely different from anything I had studied or spoken before, and, while being new and exciting, it required some major adjustments in study habits. Since first or second grade, my teachers have not only complained, but have yelled and screamed about my handwriting. If one can't master 26 English letters, imagine trying to learn several thousand Chinese characters. If I could barely write my name in English legibly, what was I supposed to do with my name in Chinese?

Well, I am now three years into Chinese. I am cofounder and president of the Chinese Society, which meets regularly to discuss China and to learn about its culture and customs. One-dimensional no more, I have discovered a subject that has truly captivated me and which I will continue to pursue.

In June the sun will set for me at St. Paul's School, and though I will miss the place, I will not regret leaving it. St. Paul's has made me want to go on. It has provided me with an atmosphere of opportunity. Equally, I have taken full advantage of that opportunity, and I hunger for more.

It is the appetite for new experiences, even more than football or Chinese, for which I am grateful. I am looking forward to more sunrises in my life.

Joanne B. Wilkinson
College: Brown University

HANDS

My father has always said that I have "brain surgeon hands," probably because they're rather large with fingers so long and thin that my school ring has to be held on with masking tape. Those who knew less about my ambitions tend to call them "basketball player hands." Of course, there is always that small minority that persist in calling them "ballet hands." (Although I danced for nine years, I no longer harbor dreams of Nutcrackers and Swan Lakes.) Under it all, I am primarily a writer; writing has allowed me to express my thoughts and ideas in every discipline, and in the words of Carl Van Vechten, "An author doesn't write with his mind, he writes with his hands."

Often, when I have a free moment, I find myself looking be-musedly at these hands of mine, and reflecting on the many things they have done. When I was a child, these hands curled themselves around a crayon to scrawl my first letters; they clutched at the han-dles of a bicycle, refusing to trust my training wheels; they arched delicately over my head in pirouettes and slid, wriggling, into softball gloves. Later, they held a pen ready to express all the ideas and ques-tions and answers that bloomed in my mind. These hands once plunged deep into the pinafore pockets of my candy-striping uni-form, emerging to write messages and lab orders, punch telephone numbers, steady syringes—all with growing ease and authority. They went with me when I babysat to earn pocket money and volunteered in my pediatrician's office, and they touched feverish foreheads and held smaller hands, trying to comfort and cheer.

They graduated to a white lab coat's pockets and learned to inject mice and create lab charts for lab data. They supported my chin dur-ing late-night studies. They hoisted my increasingly heavy knapsack to my shoulders and toted it back and forth to literary editing ses-sions, Spanish dinners, and council meetings. They donned white gloves to ring handbells with the Lambrequins, and twisted nervously behind my back while I performed; they adjusted colored lights for school performances and learned to pluck a microphone from its stand with apparent ease. They dissected pigs and worms and cows, and thought they would never be rid of the smell of formaldehyde, but they survived. They have endured mouse bites, chlorinated water, chemical spills, and poison ivy; when they needed to retreat, there was always a plush teddy bear to cuddle.

Someday, these hands will grip forceps and retractors, tense and slick; they will rake through my hair with fatigue as I sit in library carrels studying graphs and figures. Someday soon, they will hold a daisy-adorned diploma from Lincoln School, and they will hold again, as they have in the past, trophies and book awards and certifi-cates. I have confidence that they will become the hands of an M.D., with the power to heal and comfort solemnly implicit, and I have every hope that these hands will someday, thrilled and proud, touch the opened Van Wickle Gates as they enter.

COMMENTS:

Excellent, creative, original, and beautifully written! This is a student I would like to meet and know. She has a wonderful facility with words, the perfect ones to describe her thoughts. (NA)

For clarity, this essay has to be considered as one of the best. The individual is described to a "T." The reader is able to understand the maturation of the writer, see the ambition, and gain a good grasp of the strength of character. (JLM)

An excellent essay. Great image carried through in multiple instances with interesting and varied use of words and ideas that express not only her activities and goal but her philosophy of life and values. (MAH)

Compliments on taking on the risk of a difficult extended metaphor. It is consistently done, even if it becomes slightly tiresome. The playful self-deprecation of the first several paragraphs is entertaining. (TH)

Srinivas Ayyagari
College: Harvard University

A few months ago, I looked in the mirror and saw, as usual, a youngish face, which I perceived as about twelve, maybe thirteen years old. But this time I realized a deeper reason for that perception: I actually *identified* myself, my mind and personality, with the boy I was at that age. So, I struggled with the question, "How do I differ from that seventh-grader?" Distinguishing between my thoughts then and my thoughts now perplexed me: I recalled a similar way of working, intellectual capacity, and motivations. Yet the problem gnawed at me because I knew something fundamental had changed in me. After all, I was looking on that seventh-grader as a distinct personality. But why did I? What distinguished him from me? I realized eventually that the difference between that seventh-grader and me was that, since seventh grade, I had gained an outlook, a way of examining the broader world I had never considered before. The separation was clear: before the spring of tenth grade, I had lived but had never really examined life. Nigel Calder's *Einstein's Universe* finally ignited my mind with ardent inquiry.

Calder's lucid but mentally taxing explanations of Einstein's theories forced my perspective to dilate many times over. Instead of thinking in feet and miles, suddenly my fifteen-year-old mind was trying to consider millions of light years, curved space, hopping from star to black hole and back to Earth. Naturally, I was not entirely successful, but more important, the experience plunged me into a new realm of thought, visions of the vast universe floating in my mind. At first, thinking of the astronomical expanse, I delved into the obvious (and, as I quickly found, irresolvable) questions of ultimate meaning, an exceedingly elusive goal. Yet because of this errant speculation, my mind was still churning with my new view, an extremely expanded perspective about life on earth which impelled me to find out about the universal principles of existence.

Now, more than ever, I gravitated toward science. Before reading *Einstein's Universe* and undertaking my mental voyage, I had been interested in science because it was tidy, neat. Suddenly, that interest was ablaze with a passion for truth, knowledge, and not just in science. The hazy ideas that history was a study in human failure and triumph, that literature laid bare the human experience, and that science, science would reveal unifying principles of our chaotic, swirling existence burst from mist into light. In eleventh grade, the logic of evolution, the wonder of genetics, the grand design of physiology all seemed the more magnificent because they were natural consequences of chemistry. That year, inspired by the potential of biology for finding truth about man, I made my career choice: genetic research, the area in which I think I could make the greatest strides in doing the highest good as a human being, contributing to society. My physics teacher this year has taught me an even greater principle: science merely describes the real world and cannot be mistaken for absolute truth.

Ultimately, experiencing *Einstein's Universe* incited me to contemplate truly for the first time, to reevaluate my fundamental beliefs and form those which have made me more confident and peaceful than ever. Recently, I looked in the mirror at a youngish face, still a boy's, but now that face conceals a vision more expansive than the seventh-grader ever imagined.

———————

COMMENT:

In this short but powerful essay, the writer reveals much about himself and his motivations as both a learner and a maturing individual. The seventh-grader, now several years older, is impressionable and eager to grow as a scientist, as his evolving mind and sense of inquiry enable him to begin to see the connections to other disciplines. "How do I differ from that seventh-grader?" he asks, as he returns to the mirror in a compelling final paragraph. While his understanding of science has been strengthened by Calder's book, the greater achievement, he now recognizes, has been the substantial growth of his own self-awareness. While seeming somewhat idealistic, this essay is convincing in portraying the writer as a passionate student of science with realistic goals, but also as an individual earnestly in search of universal truths. (RK)

William Couper Samuelson
College: Harvard University

It is a truth universally acknowledged that weird things happen at hospitals. From the moment the automatic doors open, you are enveloped in a different world. A world of beeps, beepers, humming radiators, humming nurses, ID badges, IV bags, gift shops, shift stops, PNs, PAs, MDs, and RNs. Simply being in a hospital usually means you are experiencing a crisis of some sort. Naturally, this association makes people wary. However, I have had the unusual experience of being in a hospital without being sick—well, I did for a while.

In May 1995, I began working once a week at Massachusetts General Hospital. I imagined myself passing the scalpel to a doctor performing open heart surgery, or better yet stumbling upon the cure for cancer. It turned out, however, that those under age eighteen are not allowed to work directly with patients or doctors. I joined a lone receptionist, Mrs. Penn, who had the imposing title of "medical and informational technician." My title was "patient discharge personnel." Mrs. Penn had her own computer and possessed vast knowledge of the hospital. I had my own personal wheelchair. Manning the corner of the information desk, my wheelchair and I would be called on to fetch newly discharged patients from their rooms.

This discharge experience taught me lessons—both comical and sad—about hospital life. On one of my first days, I was wheeling out a woman when I noticed an IV needle still pressed in the back of her hand. I returned her to the nurse's station where the needle was removed without comment or apology. Another time, an elderly man approached the information desk and threatened that if I didn't let him see his wife, he would take a grenade out of his pocket and detonate it. I didn't really believe he had a grenade, but who could be sure? When the man repeated his words to Mrs. Penn, she knew exactly what to do. An immediate call for security was sounded. Sad to say, that man was not the first or last unbalanced individual to frequent Mass General while I worked there.

Nor would this be the last time I relied on Mrs. Penn. Some months later, a thirty-something man came to the desk asking for his father's room. When I looked up his computer entry, the father's name came up with the code for the morgue: deceased. Not knowing what to do, I told him my computer was down and directed him to Mrs. Penn's terminal. She broke the news and directed him to the attending physician.

Last spring, I handled the discharge of Oliver, a twelve-year-old boy undergoing chemotherapy. When I asked how he would be going home, he replied, "How do I get to the nearest subway station?" Apparently, Oliver's parents were busy and couldn't bring him home from the hospital. I gave Oliver 85 cents and walked him to the Charles/MGH subway stop. After explaining what inbound and outbound meant, I watched a frightened little boy board the train. Teenagers in my town have one thing in common: Our parents lavish us with attention, even spoil many of us. But what I saw that day opened my eyes to a life wholly different from my own.

Then life changed. On a beautiful, hot, August day, my lung collapsed. I was at a basketball camp in Cambridge when I felt a searing pain through my upper back and chest. Anyone who has had a pitchfork driven through his shoulder knows exactly how I felt. The camp trainer said not to worry; at worst, I might have an enlarged spleen, a telltale sign of "mono." The trainer had no idea what he was talking about. Next stop, the hospital.

I spent one night at Mass General, sleeping with an oxygen mask to pump my lung back up. The doctors sent me home the next morning with a sore back and no sleep: This collapsed lung was just a singular event, a one-hit wonder. Wrong. In October, my lung collapsed again. This time I spent two nights with the oxygen mask. This time when I left I was scheduled for surgery a week later. The day of surgery I saw Mrs. Penn behind the desk, but she didn't wave. I realized that with my oxygen mask I was about as recognizable as the face behind Darth Vader's mask.

Though I knew I was in good hands, my main feeling as a patient was helplessness. Nonetheless, I experienced one small triumph near the end of my stay. On the way to the CT scan, my wheelchair attendant had no clue where we were going. Not only did I know the way, I knew a shortcut. The attendant was impressed. For a moment, I was not a patient, but again part of the invisible fraternity of hospital workers.

The most consistent component of my life during that year was the hospital. When I see someone with an oxygen mask wheeled by my desk, I don't assume an attitude of indifference. I know what it is to push—and be pushed in—the wheelchair. An extended stay at the hospital helped me realize and appreciate what a normal life is.

COMMENT:

A strong introduction launches this essay effectively. The writer vividly describes his experiences as a volunteer, ranging from the moving instance with the young chemotherapy patient to other alternately routine and bizarre moments in the daily life of a major hospital. This readable and engaging essay becomes more compelling because of the writer's collapsing lung and the ensuing circumstances he himself experiences as a patient. However, it lumbers down in the closing, which unfortunately doesn't do justice to the strength of the better part of the essay. The last sentence, while an appropriate conclusion, still seems anticlimactic. (RK)

ESSAYS ON SPORTS
AND ACTIVITIES

Whitney Lee
College: Princeton University

My Choice

I could have died in that cave.

We were spelunking, and when we reached the halfway mark there was a crevasse bordering a dimly lit walkway and I slipped . . . only to be rescued by Nate and Naiji at the last second. It was the second week of cadre leadership training, the part spent in the wilderness. Cadre is a group of rising juniors and seniors, who are chosen by the AFJROTC instructors to lead the cadet corps for the following year. It is a time-tested military school tradition for the rising group of upperclassmen to practice their leadership abilities in a pressure cooker. There were mosquitoes, spiders and other insects . . . still it was nice. By the second week of cadre camp, I had been pulled, pushed and lifted by most of the guys in my squadron, in an attempt to finish our challenges: Nate and Naiji in the cave, Grant and Temple in the obstacle course and Jake for physical training. Roasting in the August sun, hoisting and being hoisted by my classmates, was a grueling experience, and I often considered giving up. Every day I had to reaffirm to myself that it was an honor to have been chosen and that I was there by my choice, not just cadre camp, but also the school.

I often reflected on my decision to come to military school, to leave behind my friends and family for a boarding school over two hundred miles away. For me, it was a welcome opportunity to begin anew, south of the Mason-Dixon line. At first, I was both excited and overwhelmed, and it was amazing being able to experience new things and put myself out there. Some things were unique to the military program, such as drill and saber team, and I had to learn to balance my extracurriculars with my schoolwork, juggling journalism and tennis with speech and debate. My days were packed, but they were no match for the nights of studying and managing the girls on my hallway, as their flight sergeant. The best part about being at my school was that I was able to try anything I wanted even when the odds were stacked against me. I loved the fact that whatever I wanted to try, I had the support of the faculty and coaching staff.

Being at R-MA has taught me many things and most were learned outside the classroom. I have learned patience by living in the dorms, perseverance by participating in sports and discipline by being a cadre member. In moments when I am exhausted and want to give up, I take comfort in the fact that R-MA has given me an amazing community of people, staff and students, in whom I can trust. As I climbed out of the cave, thankful to have emerged unharmed, I realized that my choice had been the right one.

COMMENT:

This is one of the most complete college essays I've ever read. She takes something intriguing about her application profile: the fact that she went to military school, and spins it into an essay that highlights her leadership skills while simultaneously explaining her decision to attend the school, a question that would surely have come up during interviews or at least been in the back of the minds of the admissions officers. This essay has suspense, heartfelt emotion and a touch of nostalgia for the years of high school that will soon be in her past. The writer shows maturity, in being able to look back at her high school experience and recognize the amazing opportunities that she has been afforded, and it shows the writer as a grateful person, as she thanks the teachers and coaches who helped make the experience worthwhile. (AMH)

Shelley Ledray Bornkamp
College: Washington State University

Every Little Girl's Dream

Every little girl's dream is to become a dancer. It was my dream as well.

At the age of seven I entered the dance world, and attended beginning ballet class every Saturday morning for one brief hour at Susan Cooper's School of the Dance in Mt. Vernon for little dancers. I remember how I felt at my first lesson, excited and scared, with visions of myself in the distant future as a prima ballerina in a glorious, spangled pink tutu. I continued to dance, advancing slowly by levels each year, adding then multiplying the hours that I invested at the barre. By age ten, I was dancing six hours a week, while my peers back at school were playing basketball and discussing boys. At lunch, everyone talked about what happened at practice and whether the cool boy in the math class would come to the birthday party. I lived and breathed ballet; their interests and mine no longer converged. As I increased my hours spent in the studio, my feeling of being an outcast increased proportionally.

Dancing was not a hobby to me, it became what I lived for. I did not care that I had little in common with my classmates; I enjoyed my isolation because the feeling that I had at my first ballet class was still inside me. I was going to be a professional dancer, and I would do anything to achieve that goal. That tutu changed to sweaty rehearsal clothes, leg warmers, and tattered toe shoes. Ballet lessons four times a week. The basement room in my parents' house became my practice room and the Ping-Pong table was a substitute barre. In addition to my winter work, I attended intensive summer dance camps for three years, concentrated dance training taught by professional dancers from all over the world. These summer programs not only improved my dancing skills, but also they gave me a sense of self-discipline and independence that has stayed with me to the present.

The climax of my dancing career was my acceptance to the Pacific Northwest Ballet Summer School in 1983. I was thirteen with braces and stars in my eyes. I can still remember the day I auditioned, the first time that I had been surrounded by serious competition. I thought that there was no chance of me being accepted. When the letter of acceptance came in the mail, I was shocked, amazed, and very pleased because I was accepted to the "elite" ballet school in Washington State. My success gave me the incentive to work even harder at my hometown ballet school; I knew I had to push myself in order for me to be able to compete with the other dancers.

The day finally arrived for me to go to Seattle where I would begin the six best weeks of my life. I learned new skills, a fierce independence, and continuous discipline. My urge to be a ballerina grew stronger and stronger. At the end of the six weeks, students were evaluated on their performances and a select few were offered the chance to continue through the year. I was so proud to be chosen. The decision was not hard, although I realized that I had to leave home, parents, and friends for a time. I knew that was the price I was going to pay if I really wanted to dance.

I moved to my new home with Debra Hadly, one of the principal ballerinas in the company. I began my new regime: three hours a day, six days a week, at the same time attending a demanding all-girls Catholic School, Holy Name Academy. It was a special year, not only for me but also for the Pacific Northwest Ballet, because the company worked feverishly to produce the world premiere performance of Maurice Sendak's *The Nutcracker Suite,* a re-creation of story, costumes, scenery, sets, and choreography. Without much confidence I attended the auditions, hoping for a part, any part. My wish was granted with two fairly demanding roles: part of the Calvary and a Scrim Mouse. I was ecstatic! Even though I would have to spend every weekend in Seattle for rehearsals, I did not care. I lived and breathed the exciting world of professional ballet. Opening night was sheer magic. Exhausted but delirious with accomplishment, I did my homework in backstage corners in between rehearsals.

Unfortunately, the *Nutcracker* also marked the beginning of my failure as a dancer. I began to worry more about my competition than about my self-improvement. My body began to take the shape of a normal teenager rather than that of a dancer. I found that I really missed being connected with my mother, a crucial part of a young teenage girl's life. By mid-April I was depressed; I had put on fifteen pounds and dancing no longer made me happy. It was time for me to do some serious evaluating of my situation. I met with the head of the Ballet School and with my mother many times, and I finally concluded that it was time to give up dance. This was the hardest decision of my life. It led to a good year of finding a "new" Shelley. I felt that someone had taken away the past fourteen years of my life and I had to start all over. It was an extremely hard time for me, but with the encouraging support of my mother and close friends, I pulled out of it, I worked hard to become a normal teenaged girl. I learned to like football games, parties, cheerleading, friends, and good times. I also learned to like myself once more.

When I look back at what I had to go through and what I gave up to become a dancer and then at my decision to leave the world of ballet, I wonder how I made it through my fifteenth year. I have come out of that black period of my life with a great many personal strengths. I have talents other than dancing; I am a strong, independent, and caring person. I have met with depression and have turned my failure into success. Somewhere in the back corner of my head lives a pink tutu, but my years as a dancer are behind me and I am ready to take on new challenges.

COMMENTS:

Well-organized and generally well-written essay about a very important part of the writer's life. The subsequent emotional conflict it created for her and the traumatic decision she had to make reveals her strength of character and her eagerness to look forward. I think the same story could have been told in fewer words, however, and perhaps this is its only weakness. (NA)

Shelley relates a profoundly significant personal story, somewhat tragic given the way she portrays her long journey into dance, and then the way it became so suddenly rerouted. I feel that I'd like to hear more about the outcome, having heard so much about the lead-in. She pokes a lot into the last two paragraphs and well, but less profoundly. However, it is an excellent essay and very interesting tale. (MAH)

A decent, well-done, but workmanlike essay; it is ultimately dull. She would have done better to describe the dancing and its impact than to recount in lockstep chronology her autobiography in dance. This is straight history without images. (TH)

The "decision" essay is often very predictable. This one is no exception. While the outcome was not in doubt, Shelley is able to portray a dedicated dancer, and we get a good picture of Shelley's personality. The dedication is evident as is the pain of the decision, but also is the knowledge that it was the correct one. (JLM)

Terrance Darnell Moore
College: Harvard University

As students go through high school, too often they are absorbed in too many superfluous things and lose the value of giving back to their school and community. I contrarily believe that my high school career should be exemplified by excellent academics as well as my commitment to my school and community. An aspect of this belief that I am very much proud of along with my exceptional academic performance is my participation in Boy Scouts, where after eight years I accomplished the rank of Eagle Scout. This event is a milestone in my life because of the values it has taught me, the virtue of service it has instilled in me, and the foundation it has laid.

During my experience in scouting, not only have I been taught many practical things but many valuable life lessons as well. Scouting has shaped me as a leader and young man. It has taught me responsibility, leadership, and how to work with others. It has also instilled numerous values including hard work, which is evident in my achieving Eagle Scout. I have learned through many experiences how to work with a culturally diverse group of people and still strive to achieve a common goal. But along with my own enlightening, I am most proud of the privilege to communicate with and guide younger scouts to achieving what I have and to grow into men.

Service is an essential asset to scouting which is constantly stressed. Through the virtue of service, I have always been connected to my community. I have led and completed many service projects and activities including the building of two bookshelves for my church Sunday school department. Along with this project I feel I have served also by my example. Many children have told me how they look up to me and my actions. I feel that this kind of positive influence is a much needed and irreplaceable contribution to today's society. My service is especially important to me because I believe that one's accomplishments mean little if no one else is inspired to do the same by their actions.

The reason I have stayed so persistent with scouting throughout the years is in my belief that it would lay a strong foundation for my future. The rank of Eagle Scout marks the achieving of a milestone that few are able to reach because of its many obstacles. These obstacles that I have surpassed will contribute to my future endeavors. My exposure to the diversity that scouting introduced has equipped me with the ability to lead and communicate in and with a team and will be essential in later successes in life. This exposure has also helped me to gain a broader understanding of the world around me and my place in it. The list of scouting's contributions to me is endless but has surely laid a bridge to future prosperity in my life.

Many people see me as a talented and gifted young man of many dimensions that has a great influence on my peers. This young man is derived from many factors, so choosing one most important only partially tells my story. But of these factors, scouting would most likely be one I hold especially important in my extracurricular background. This factor has such importance because of the values it has taught me, the virtue of service it has instilled in me, and the foundation it has laid. As a prospective student at Harvard College, it would be detrimental to miss out on a young man of my caliber as a contributing member of your institution.

COMMENTS:

This essay, although formulaic, is well written, descriptive and illustrates passion for Boy Scouts. The essay is also unapologetic as a brag fest of the student's achievements. While this does convey confidence, it adds to the length and once this is stripped away, there is little substance. I would suggest this writer knock out anything that is already elsewhere in the application: academics, community contribution, description of scouting and its value. It is a given that scouting stands on service; detailing this takes valuable time from this young fellow's stint in the driver's seat. College admissions people are smart; they know what scouting involves and do not require a dissertation. Please, dear boy, tell me more about your Eagle Scout project. The writer states children look up to him, but I need an example. He touts being gifted and a great influence, but again an example is missing. The student concludes with the challenge to take a stand and admit him, yet the broad generalized perspective offers nothing to the soul of this young man. Unfortunately the yes factor is missing. (BLB)

Joseph Libson
College: Princeton University

At the risk of transforming this application into a tract on the wonders of wrestling, I nonetheless wish to discuss my recent vacation through hell. Hell, by the way, is not located under the earth. No, the current residence of Satan is Edinboro, Pennsylvania. Hell opens for two weeks every summer and the operators slap on the snappy title "J. Robinson's Intensive Wrestling Camp." The daily routine for this camp is so rigorous that graduation with honors consists of receiving a black shirt with the daily schedule inscribed on the back in mute testament to the existence of this habitation of fallen angels. Each camp session the dropout/casualty rate varies from 25 to 50% (even with an avowed policy of no refunds). I cannot describe the total impact of this place but I can sure as J. Robinson's Intensive Wrestling Camp try.

We wake at 6 A.M. every morning. If your group is lucky you lift weights, if not you run. This exercise is not a typical long-distance endurance run, but rather sadistic combinations of endurance and sprint running. One section, deceptively called the 'Buddy Carry,' involved running with a partner about my size. The instructor ran us down a long country road about three miles from camp. At his signal, I carried my partner on my back at as fast a pace as I could muster. At the halfway mark we switched and he carried me. The indescribable pain that accompanied this operation almost broke me. But, of course, the "almost" is what the camp is all about. The run lasted an hour and a half. We showered, ate breakfast, and crawled back to our rooms to catch a nap before Technique Session. Technique Session is a two-hour "easy" practice that is as difficult as normal wrestling practice at most schools. After the first session I was convinced that I didn't want to see the "hard" practice. I was right. Hard practice is live wrestling for two hours. I have never been so tired as after a hard practice. But, it made the technique sessions seem really easy. I never got used to hard practice. Every day panic would creep into my thoughts. "This is never going to end. I can't keep this up any longer." Invariably I survived the practice and staggered to shower and dinner, after which came the fourth session. This was almost a repeat of the morning session in difficulty but was preceded by a motivational talk, during which most of us practiced sleeping standing up. Days passed until finally, on the schedule board, in the section devoted to the Hard Practice drills, appeared the words

RED FLAG DAY

Curious, how such innocuous words could inspire such terror. The rumors of Red Flag Day had been circulating throughout the camp since day two. When it finally arrived, dread filled every wrestler's heart. One hour and forty minutes of nonstop wrestling was assigned, with no breaks or instruction periods where a wrestler might catch his breath. If regular hard practice was difficult, this was surely impossible. But, we did it, most of us, and we did it twice. On the last day, before the end of the camp session we had another Red Flag Day; this one was two hours long. To graduate with honors a wrestler had to have 500 points. Everyone in camp started with 800 points, which could be lost through bad room checks, discipline problems, or not working hard enough during practice. Two minuses and one plus were awarded during every practice. I have never worked so hard for anything as the one plus I received in one practice during that hellish two weeks. The last exercise of the camp was a twelve-mile run. It was unbelievably easy, for we all knew that after the run IT WAS ALL OVER AND WE COULD GO HOME.

In spite of my sarcasm, it is probably obvious that the camp was one of the greatest experiences in my life. It taught me that there are very few limits to what achievement a person can attain. Having the coach yell, "Sprint, dammit!" when all that you desperately desire to do is fall down and sleep right there not only conditions your body, it also disciplines your mind. This mental strength has enabled me to work harder at anything that I try. One cannot endure an experience like that camp and not be the better for it. I am no exception.

COMMENT:

This essay is good because, although the experience occurred at a wrestling camp, the writer avoids the trap of letting wrestling become the focus of the essay, but just barely. What this piece does do is show that the writer can endure physical hardship and pain without quitting, over a relatively long period of time. In that sense the scope of this essay is a bit one-dimensional. (AST)

Gregory Lippman
College: Princeton University

There is a certain smell when you walk into a gymnasium, a hermetic, airless kind of smell. A smell of leather, of shellacked parquet floors, of old sweat. I like that smell.

Basketball has always been for me a lot more than simply a release at the end of the day or just another of the seasonal sports. The intensity, the speed, the sudden drama inherent to basketball is matched by few other games. I love basketball not because I am especially good at it; on the contrary, I fit perfectly the stereotype of the "preppie" player: no speed, no leaping ability, no quickness. I have a decent outside shot, and that has carried me to the varsity level at a high school with an unremarkable basketball tradition.

But basketball has that ineffable quality about it, that certain thing which I find it hard to pin down but which keeps me coming back to the court day after day. Maybe it's the power and the dexterity all wrapped up into one, or perhaps that feeling of fluidity and constant motion as the ball flits from player to player in a kind of schoolyard ballet. And ballet is not an inappropriate word here, because basketball is the most graceful of all competitive sports. I know of no sight more graceful than a man, weaving and bobbing through defenders, to suddenly, forcefully, move toward the basket, arm outstretched, and lay the ball gently in the hoop.

But those are just the surface attractions. The real allure of the game comes for me in other ways. It comes in that tight pull of pride when you and a teammate combine a bit of passing fancy to set up an easy score, slapping five gently as you run back downcourt to set up on defense. It comes from the eye contact across the court, to know instinctively and instantly what your teammate is going to do. When that unspoken communication exists, the game suddenly becomes easy. The joining of wills, the confluence of desire between myself and my teammates is the most satisfying part of basketball. In all the other sports I have played, nowhere is the sense of team so immediate and blunt. The absence of it is felt just as strongly as its presence. And when it, that indescribable it, is there, the rush of emotion is unmatchable. Teamwork can be talked about, diagrammed, planned out ad infinitum, but it never comes that way. But that slap on the hand and that look across a crowded court, that's where it comes from and that's where I go looking for it every time I step on to the court.

_____

COMMENT:

It isn't terribly unlike the hundreds of "sports essays" a committee is prone to receive, but in its own way, this one is fresh and interesting. The writer avoids cliché and, particularly with its use of the term "schoolyard ballet," expresses his feelings toward the game in creative, original fashion. The essay is concise, and well organized. It combines some measure of formality with an equal measure of informality—making the piece entirely appropriate for a college essay, but also highly readable. Not profound, but nonetheless effective. (RJO)

John C. Martin
College: Yale University

WHAT ACTIVITY OR INTEREST HAS MEANT THE MOST TO YOU? WHY?

I have never been able to convince my nine-year-old sister to change television channels. As a fourth-year debater, supposedly gifted in the arts of persuasion, this knowledge should be disturbing to me. Yet, for some strange reason, it isn't. While I've tried very hard to discover the reason for my relaxed attitude toward this problem, until very recently I couldn't find a solid answer. At first I thought my attitude might indicate a lack of the "killer instinct" that is necessary to any good high school debater, for my interest in Lincoln-Douglas debate has never been limited to the numbers in my won and loss columns. Yet, I would be the first to admit that I have found victory to be thrilling and defeat to be agonizing. Furthermore, when the issue at hand deals not with the propositions of great value found in "Philosophies of Hate Should Be Suppressed for the Good of Society" but rather with the more mundane concerns presented in "Dallas Reruns Should be Suppressed in Favor of Monday Night Football," a lack of enthusiasm might well be expected.

Perhaps my problems with my sister arise from a lack of logical argument, for part of my enjoyment of debate stems from my passion for rational discussions of the political and moral philosophies of such giants as Emmanuel Kant and John Stuart Mill. In contrast to this, my arguments with my sister are anything but logical, calling on "family rules" that are often invented on the spot and are, more often than not, unfairly biased toward the inventing party. Fortunately, while debate is theoretically based on rational argument, it has also provided me with experience in dealing with such irrationality. Take, for instance, the resolution "It is Better to be a Dissatisifed Socrates than a Satisfied Pig" in which many debaters ignored all possibility of metaphor and argued the value of a somewhat unhappy, and very dead Greek philosopher versus that of a happy, well-fed quadruped rolling in the mud. Other examples lie in the hypotheticals in which Mr. T goes back in time to defeat Socrates in a boxing match, thus proving that "Conflict Limits Humanity," or in debates where crucial arguments rest on quotes from "The Saurus" or "Ibid." With rational argument thus eliminated as a possibility, it seemed as if my quest for an explanation might be utterly fruitless.

As is the case with most debaters, I had failed to find a reason for my lack of disappointment because I had forgotten something elemental. In this case, I had forgotten what was, in many ways, the most important difference between Lincoln-Douglas debate and arguments over television rights. As a Lincoln-Douglas debater, I am constantly reminded of the fact that I am a member of a team. The process of developing arguments is such that it cannot possibly be done by one person alone. Brainstorming sessions and constant informal arguing are a necessary precondition to the proper preparation of a resolution. It is here where I have played my most important and most enjoyable role. While my personal won/loss record may not be as fantastic as those racked up by many of my fellow debaters, the record of those team arguments that I have played a critical part in developing is a source of great personal pride. While it is always satisfying to know that I have done well myself, perhaps my most satisfying moments as a member of the Hearn (Regis' pet name for its speech and debate society) have been those in which I have seen a fellow Hearn member who had turned to me for help in debate use my help to go on and win a state championship or other major award. While I may be personally hurt by debate decisions that didn't go my way, the satisfaction of being a crucial part of a winning team more than makes up for such disappointments. Thus, it was no surprise that I was not terribly upset by losing battles over television control with my youngest sister. After all, I have two other sisters, and, as a team, we're unstoppable.

COMMENTS:

Although this essay is well written and cleverly presented and, at the same time, does give the reader some insight into this young man's thoughts and feelings, I feel he spends an inordinate amount of time describing a couple of personal interests or views. (TG)

A very readable approach to what could have been a dull subject. The last paragraph is especially good because Martin finally emerges from behind debate topics and even hints at a little sense of humor. (JWM)

Kimberly I. McCarthy
College: Brown University

"Here she comes again. Just like always—running in, breathless, a stack of books in her arms. She throws the books on top of me and glides onto my bench, screeching to a stop in its center. Then she gently lays her hands in position on my keys, and sighs. 'I really shouldn't be here,' she tells me, 'I have chem to study, and a creative writing paper, and eighty lines of Latin, and a watercolor, and . . .' She begins to play. It's my favorite, the Moonlight Sonata. It always reminds me of her—gentle and loving yet deeply passionate. Her fingers press tenderly at first as if my keys were ivory eggshells and ebony velvet. Then she is swept up in the tide of her own emotions and begins to play louder, stronger, faster, her fingers working furiously, faster and faster and then over. She caresses my keyboard, eyes closed, then gasps. 'Oh, God! It's 3:15! I'm going to be late to karate!' She jumps up and runs out the door without so much as a glance over her shoulder—but that's all right. She'll be here tomorrow. Maybe not at the same time, maybe with different books. But she'll be here. She told me—no matter how hard the courses get, no matter how smothering the work, no matter how little time, she could never give me up. It's wonderful to be loved."

<hr/>

COMMENTS:

Enchanting essay which reveals the writer's flair. It says a great deal about the student in very few, simply stated, and carefully chosen phrases. Wish there were more essays like this one to read. It demonstrates that "less" can be excellent. (NA)

I like the brevity; the whimsy; and it's a good glimpse of who this person is and what her interests and commitments are. (MAH)

This piece is beautiful. There is a wonderful expression to it, and yet it is short and to the point. One gets a good picture of the girl and her emotions. (JLM)

Mitch S. Neuger
College: Yale University

CYCLING

I came home from school, inhaled two bagels and a glass of orange juice, squirmed into a new pair of black Lycra chamois-lined cycling shorts, pumped up my tires, and carried my bike down the front steps to the driveway. Some days I rode south, up a hill, across a street and onto the bike path. Or north, past the polo field, along the river. I sang to myself, watched the odometer, and daydreamed, looking up occasionally at the trees whose leaves were just losing their summer green. In an hour and a half I returned home and recorded my distance and average speed on a homemade chart on my wall.

I began this routine in September of my junior year, a week after returning from my summer job as a bicycle mechanic in Massachusetts. I was training, preparing myself for an organized ten-week cross-country bike trip that was eight months away.

Miles accumulated: fifty . . . one hundred . . . two hundred fifty . . . six hundred. When the oak trees hung on to their very last leaves, I pedaled inside on a stationary bicycle and joined the weight-lifting club at school. Six days a week I exercised until one day in December I lost all feeling in my big toe. The numbness persisted; I loosened my toe straps; I stopped exercising; I called my pediatrician, a sports physiologist, and a neurosurgeon; I wrote to *Bicycling* magazine. A new pair of cycling shoes solved the problem. On a mild day in February, I took my new shoes for a ride in the park. I returned shortly with a flat tire and deflated spirits.

Miles paid off in more pain and frustration. In April I developed Osgood-Schlatter's disease, a tendonitis of the knees. Again I consulted unconcerned doctors and gym teachers, read health encyclopedias and *Prevention* magazine, rested, stretched, and took vitamins. Suddenly it was spring. In just two months I would be riding "seventy to one hundred miles a day" on a bicycle loaded with fifty pounds of clothing, food, and camping gear.

I told none of my classmates what I was doing. I was afraid of impressing them with my ambitious plans and then not following through because of knee trouble or illness. And would anyone believe that I, a scrawny kid, a failed soccer player, was going to pedal my bike four thousand three hundred miles? I scarcely believed it myself; I was sure that some injury, some accident, would render months of training useless.

As the dogwoods bloomed, my enthusiasm wilted. The road was so familiar, progress was barely noticeable, and I had run out of daydreams. My new bicycle, which had arrived completely unassembled in three boxes, made a new noise every day. One day an older cyclist caught up to me; he wanted to coast and chat. I told him after a while that I was training to ride across America. "That'll take some serious riding," he said with a laugh. The bike tour brochure gave two prerequisites for this trip: "You must be in *great* shape" and "You must *love* to bicycle!" When I had first read about the trip over a year before, I believed I could do it. But now I wondered if I were meeting some personal challenge or just inflicting punishment upon myself.

And then one magic day in gym class, I was trying desperately to do a handstand when my teacher said, "Hey, your legs are getting bigger, you been working out or something?" On the road that afternoon, I met a young couple who was riding from California to Maine. They told me that the TransAmerica Trails, which I would be riding, were wonderful. Every hill I climbed on the way home that day was an Appalachian pass; every headwind was a Colorado breeze. I rode up my driveway exhausted, but restless and excited.

During the first week of summer, I began to pack—among other things, a flashlight, five new tee-shirts, and my cycling shorts, now tattered, the chamois dry and cracked. I disappeared every morning with my bike and a snack and reappeared late afternoon, sweaty and mosquito-bitten. I constantly wondered about the other kids who signed up for the trip, if they were somehow more prepared and confident.

On the morning before my trip, my thigh muscle tightened up. My doctor was on vacation; the library was closed; I decided that I'd be back home within the week. But by midnight, my bicycle was sealed in a cardboard box along with an empty journal and a bottle of vitamins. I lay on my bed, exhausted but not sleepy, thinking about tomorrow as I had for many months past.

COMMENT:

The "cyclist" in this essay presents us with a picture of himself that is rich in the details of his physical and emotional struggle to meet his commitment to the summer trip. In the process his qualities of determination (sticking it out to the end), resourcefulness (building his own bike), and "heart" are made completely apparent to the reader in subtle but powerful ways. This essay was written by a keen observer of the world he lives in, and a person whose self-awareness is very high. (AST)

Christine Richardson
College: Princeton University

My dance lessons began in the seventh grade. It was not watching a performance at the Kennedy Center that prompted me to beg for the lessons; instead it was watching a friend's ballet class one evening that sparked my enthusiasm. I wanted to fly through the air with pink satin pointe shoes on my feet.

When doing my homework, I often look at a poster that hangs on the wall across the room from my desk. Six pairs of dance shoes line the bottom of the gray poster and in the middle, written in large white letters, reads, "Dance is the only art wherein we ourselves are the stuff of which it is made."

I believe in that quote. In dance there are no formulas like those in my physics book, formulas that always work. Dance is not the pointe shoes, or the jazz shoes, or the steps; it comes from within the dancer. It is her style, her interpretation that makes a dancer unique.

I now take ballet, jazz, and tap lessons, and each type of dance has many similar steps; but the steps are merely the technique; dance is the overall result of style. I can do a jeté, and depending on my execution, the music, or my mood, I can look like a sea nymph or a sports car. Shakespeare said, "All the world is a stage . . . ," but when I perform, the stage becomes all the world. The costumes, makeup, lights, and choreography draw the audience's attention to the dancer; for three or thirty minutes, the dance is the entire world. There is only one chance to do the steps I want to. I know that I have no second opportunity.

Dance is also discipline. Serious dancing means having to make all my muscles work while looking poised and graceful. Dancing can be exhausting and frustrating as sweat drips and muscles cramp. However, at other times, I actually feel the sensation of flying, flying through the air with the pink satin pointe shoes or the black leather jazz shoes. Dance, to me, is flying without wings.

COMMENT:

The author does not tell—but shows—her love for dance. She is wise to avoid using the essay to list her accomplishments in dance, and instead illustrates for us how she feels about it. In this way, we gain some insight into her personality, as opposed to receiving a list of accomplishments. The essay is concise, thoughtful, and entertaining. Well done.

Alexander P. Nyren
College: Harvard University

Gripping the rungs of the rope-and-stick ladder tightly, I had managed to get halfway up the tree before the panic set in. I looked up: twenty feet to go. I decided to wait where I was for a bit to slow my racing mind and heartbeat.

"So much for having conquered my fear of heights," I joked. "Is this thing insured?"

This was the notorious high ropes course on the Dalton senior Peer Leadership retreat. After applying, twenty-two members of the junior class are selected to become Peer Leaders. These students are paired and given a group of freshmen the following fall. We help them to adjust to life in high school, advising them on sex, drugs, academics, or whatever else comes up. The first rite of Leadership training was a three-day session in late August. (The freshmen would come on a similar trip with us a week later, which we would run ourselves.) The purposes of this retreat were to familiarize us with the activities, engage us in discussion, help us bond as a group, and of course, have fun.

Climbing around on wires forty feet in the air, I discovered, was not my idea of fun. I finished ascending the ladder and stepped onto the first wire. The "facilitators" called this section of the course the "Multi-vines." I called it torture. Some misguided neuron forced me to look down. I began to scream like a banshee. I was, shall we say, uncomfortable. I refused to step away, grasping the security of the tree instead. I did not doubt my ability to complete the course, but I did not wish to endure the pain, struggle, and potential embarrassment along the way. I screamed that I wanted to come down, right then, no joke.

But what would happen if I climbed back down? What would my fellow Peer Leaders think of me? How could I ask the freshmen to push themselves if I was not willing to test my own limits? How could I respect myself after such a debacle? I felt a surge of helplessness beginning to overcome me. While I am used to challenging myself intellectually, I usually try to avoid unfamiliar physical tasks. I am not the "Outward Bound" sort of person; my mother says that this is genetic. It was not the exertion that was bothering me, either; years of soccer practice and working out had conditioned me. I was nervous about testing my physical skills in an area in which I had essentially no experience. But I would not let myself back down that ladder.

I forged ahead onto the wire, yelling with all of my might, wondering if I was mentally prepared for this task. "The Vines" was only the first of the course's eight parts! Someone down below yelled at me to stop thinking and walk, and I realized that I was almost to the next tree. This was not half bad! I even started to enjoy myself. Completing the last stage, the zip line, was perhaps the most relieving and exhilarating moment of my life.

Except, that is, for putting my feet back on the ground. I was elated, and not just because I was out of that horribly chafing harness, or because I was no longer what seemed to be two seconds away from a bloody demise. I was proud. Having challenged myself would enable me to encourage the freshmen honestly when they confronted their own personal challenges.

More than that, I knew that the self-assurance this experience (ordeal?) had helped me to develop would be indispensable when I faced the challenges of the future. The ropes course was a seemingly insurmountable problem which was indeed solvable when broken into several sections. While my academic life in high school has been quite challenging, I know that it cannot compare with college, graduate school, or (gasp!) real life. Completing the ropes course in relative style was an important personal accomplishment; never before had I felt so unsure of my capabilities, never again would I feel quite so panicked. I now have confidence in my ability not only to do what comes easily to me, but to overcome what might seem to be the most ornery of obstacles. Outward Bound here I come! Yeah, right.

COMMENT:

The problem here is that most of the essay deals with the negatives of the experience that the writer is describing rather than the positives. The writer challenged himself; he succeeded in finishing the course. He had never felt so uncertain of his abilities before. OK, but—somehow I'm not convinced that this experience will necessarily translate into any other area of his life. It feels like an essay I've read often before. (MR)

Dani Ruran
College: Amherst College

Rose was a physically unattractive and overweight elderly spinster. She lived with her sister in a little white house, where she often gave music lessons to young violinists. The zenith of her day was when she sat in her living room on her black piano bench, leaned over the violin in her lap, and instructed a child on the essence of bowing and fingering.

I was six years old when I first met Rose, and I had just moved to West Hartford. I had begun playing the violin several months prior to our move and was very concerned about changing teachers. My first instructor was young, beautiful, kind, and patient. She was impressed by my love of music and with my willingness to practice; I had looked forward to our weekly lessons.

My mother searched for a replacement for June. She was told that Rose Kleman was the best teacher of violin for young children and made an appointment for me to meet her.

Rose arranged to interview me at her home. I took one look at this new and very different-looking teacher and promptly forgot all the music I had learned. I could not play a single note. But, she began to talk to me about music, asked me to call her "Rose," and brought me into one of the most heart-warming and productive relationships of my life.

As the weeks passed and we became better acquainted, Rose added dimension to the life of my family. With both sets of grandparents living too far away for frequent contact, she became another grandmother to my sisters and me and another mother to my parents.

The experience she gained through working with so many young children enabled her to give me guidelines for life while she helped me to develop as a violinist. She told me that I was "almost grown up now" and that I was to carry my own violin up the steps to her fourth-floor studio. When I had difficulty facing a performance, she would say, "You will do it," and I did. She taught me how to budget my time and how to balance my daily activities. Because of her rare dedication and true caring, she often gave me lessons at her home, for which she did not charge.

One Yom Kippur, the concertmaster of the Hartford Symphony (who would soon become my teacher) played Max Bruch's *Kol Nidre* in our synagogue. I remember sitting near Rose and looking up at her face in sheer delight, sharing two common joys with her—the spiritual mysteries of religious and musical fulfillment.

During the week of my tenth birthday, my family visited relatives in Philadelphia. On our third day there, we were awakened in the early morning by a telephone call. I saw my mother's eyes redden as she held the phone to her ear. When she hung up, she broke the news slowly. Rose had died unexpectedly. Soon, my whole family was in tears. I remember the distraught look on my little sister's face and the puzzled look on my cousin's as he peeked through the open door, trying to find out what had happened.

I vowed to remember Rose, her teachings and her kindness. I began taking lessons with my new teacher, the concertmaster, and I continue to work hard at the violin. Whenever I enter a competition, I think of Rose before playing my first note. I hear her saying, "You will do it," and I do. And silently, I dedicate my performance to her.

I would like to spend another evening with Rose. I would like to see the joy on her face as she learned that she had helped me to grow, both musically and personally, and heard how I was continuing what she had begun.

COMMENT:

Obviously, this is written with sincere, heartfelt emotion, but although it reveals that the writer is sensitive and musically inclined, we don't learn much about the writer herein. (Perhaps that was not specifically the purpose of this essay question.) At any rate, it is a highly personalized response, and a description of a unique relationship. I do wish the writer had employed additional specific instances of anecdotes that would have further illustrated what this lovely person Rose was like. The one example of the concert at the synagogue is effective—but seems isolated in the essay. I'd call this a B+ essay that with one or two more specific recollections could become an "A." (RJO)

Peter Urkowitz
College: University of Chicago

I wanted to draw in the rain. It was not really rain, just a lot of people in raincoats trying to make each other believe that they were hiding from the sky for a reason. Well, maybe it was a bit wet, but no one seemed to notice that there were many more people on the streets than there would have been had it really been raining. Real rain would drown out the city with noise, wash pigeons into drains, sweep cats straight into the river, tip over garbage cans and float the trash away, and leave red marks wherever raindrops hit bare skin. This barely had distinguishable drops; there seemed a strange continuity to this rain, as if it were an extraordinarily dense mist, or a very airy river that was flowing out of the sky and oozing onto the ground rather than, as real rain would have done, attacking the ground like a machine gun.

It wasn't even dark. When I came out of the school building I had to blink my eyes, to let them adjust, in exactly the same way that I had almost every day since school had begun. I had my umbrella open, of course. Everybody had their umbrellas open. Everybody was wearing a raincoat, too. Everybody was hunched forward, shoulders tensed. None of them cast a shadow, but that was their own fault. Of course, I had no shadow either. Was I afraid of embarrassment?

Yet this light, from a sun ineffectively hidden by translucent clouds, was interesting in a way. When figures are equally lit from all directions, they become weird creatures, gray and colorless without becoming less lively. It was the illusion of rain that made them less lively. I thought about how I could draw objects without shading, how to describe contours on a uniformly gray mass.

Looking up, I was distracted by the view down the street. If drawing objects without details seemed hard, how much harder would infinite details be? As I looked down the street, and the facades of buildings formed unreproduceable angles toward the horizon, and the windows were placed in patterns so complex that it would take days to sort them out, and every iron railing on the steps was a work of art, I felt like crying.

I was quiet. Around me the city was unhurried but loud, except at moments when it grew silent and rushed past me. I felt the urge to paint the whole scene with one explosive stroke of a brush. It was clear before me, a true vision calling me out to be expressed, by the sudden release of boundless energy this vision could be communicated to the world. I didn't move. The energy was there, perhaps, but only if it were controlled and manipulated could this vision, if it were such, be expressed. That was the root of real power. The people I know who are powerful intellects all have this ability: to sustain their energy over extended periods, directing it to their purpose.

Only at rare moments do I feel intellectually powerful enough to sustain an artistic vision over the time that it takes to actually execute a drawing. Only when the execution itself requires a further insight can I remain in the state of excitement that the original idea provokes. As I improve in skill I find that this further insight happens more and more often, for I am more able to approach each line, each brush stroke, with renewed spontaneity.

In writing, this spontaneity is easier to achieve, for it is more obviously necessary. Because any piece of writing is broken up into paragraphs and sentences, and by the progression of an action or an idea, it is impossible to conceptualize the entirety of a piece before it is physically written. At the very least, word and syntax choices must be made as they arise. At best, a work grows in the writing to be better than its conception. And because each word presents a new challenge, I often feel the excitement which prompts me to begin drawing only after I begin writing. As I write I build momentum and confidence, until I reach a peak of concentration. All barriers to achievement seem to melt before me, and words and ideas come forth.

It is at these moments that I feel intellectually and artistically powerful: subtle and sophisticated, exercising immense control over a boundless force.

COMMENT:

This is a stunning piece for several reasons. First, the opening encloses the reader in a world where there are no points of reference. This world of shadowless rain and misty sun, of raincoats and tears and of questions and explanations, is evocative and disorienting, but gripping. Second, had he ended with the usual poem I'm not sure the essay would work, but he comments on it, revealing his ability to step back from the artistic piece and be reflective. (PT)

IDEA ESSAYS

Lindsay Grain Carter
College: Mount Holyoke College

> "Southern trees bear a strange fruit,
> Blood is on the leaves and blood at the root."
> "Strange Fruit"

This work of music is a haunting tale of the old Jim Crow South in the aftermath of the Reconstruction period in America. Unsettling, indeed and that is certainly the point. In 1939, the legendary jazz songstress Billie Holiday recorded this protest song as a way of calling attention to the horrible lynchings of black men. Miss Holiday's signature tune "Strange Fruit" whispers the imagery of death. The lyrics paint a disturbing scene against the backdrop of the pastoral countryside of old world antebellum mansions with manicured lawns, juxtaposed with scarred human flesh dangling in the trees as a soft breeze rustles and a butterfly takes flight. This strange fruit yields a different kind of harvest, a bitter crop, a human stain amidst refined genteel manners and delightful Southern charm. The significance of this song provokes raw emotion. It captures the unspoken cancer gripping Southern communities infested with hatred against blacks and the racist acts of violence committed during this reign of terror. The madness invokes a portrait of the darkness in humanity. This fruit smells of a nasty stench; charred bodies mangled while buzzards pluck the skin through a noose tied forcibly around their limp frames. Billie Holiday expresses her sorrow and anger against lynching and the perpetrators that committed such heinous crimes against black men. This song unsettles me because it conjures up frightening images of blacks cruelly tortured and the fate to which they succumbed. Listening to the sad melody becomes a harrowing ordeal for the audience and the artist.

Every time I hear this song, I envision the slave shackles of my African ancestors and the price they paid for my freedom. Equality and racial justice are my inheritance in this land of liberty. This song demonstrates the depravity of the Klu Klux Klan and their Southern campaign of terror to annihilate individual freedom. Feelings of frustration, poverty, depression and anxiety offer a sober image masking the torture and heart wrenching pain that segregated blacks endured from the wrath in America. "Strange Fruit" becomes a powerful example of blues music depicting the horrors of lynching, yet the word never appears in the lyrics. It is a poignant illustration of a protest song advocating for social change and human rights. This is no rare feat, as social activism was not promoted or tolerated in the 1930's. Billie Holiday risked her fame by recording a song that offended the few and raised the consciousness of many.

COMMENT:

The writer critiques a controversial protest song of harrowing subject matter. The writer's use of the word "unsettling" describes perfectly the emotion that envelops her as she details social injustice conveyed through art. The writer does not rely on the controversy to convey her connection, rather the historical perspective that binds her to the song. The reader is treated to a beautifully written essay that elevates the writer and reveals her pride and heritage. (BLB)

Jennifer L. Cooper
College: Harvard University

I have of late been thinking about numbers quite a lot, the number one in particular. The abstract quality of numbers fascinates me, and I've been trying to relate them to other abstract concepts, like wholeness and love and perfection.

For example, a glass—Glass A. If Glass A has a small chip in it, it isn't *less* than one glass. If it has a small lump on it, it isn't *more* than one glass. The glass is still one; it is one of itself. It is a perfect Glass A.

This inspires further thought. It is impossible ever to have duplicate Glass A's. The ideal glass exists only in theory. How, then, can two things ever have enough in common to be called two? Put two glasses together and all you have is two ones. The ideal two does not exist. There is no such thing as the ideal two.

I found this concept very disturbing. The ramifications of the non-existence of the number two would be extensive. How could there be true love without two? I asked friends, teachers; no one had the answer.

Fortunately, I came across a solution to this problem just recently, in e. e. cummings' poem, "if everything happens that can't be done." He sets up the idea of the individual one with lines like "there's nothing as something as one" and "one's everyanything." He then reveals that two ones are involved with each other—in love. He unites these ideas, wrapping it up beautifully in the last stanza:

> we're anything brighter than even
> the sun
> (we're everything greater
> than books
> might mean)
> we're everyanything more than
> believe
> (with a spin
> leap
> alive we're alive)
> we're wonderful one times one

One *times* one! It makes so much sense. We don't generally think of multiplication using two *objects*. Usually, we think, "One apple one *time*"—equals one apple. However, Punnett squares have shown that multiplying one horse by one donkey will yield one mule. Decidedly different from either of the originals, it nevertheless combines characteristics of both into one being.

So it must be with people. The love of two individuals, while independent of one another, blends together to form one love—*their* love. People speak of "our love" or "the love between us" or "the love that we share." The two ones multiply to equal one, but that final one is different, seems richer, *fuller* than either of the originals.

The implications are intriguing. I had no idea that numbers could mean so much. It's a paradox, because mathematics is the ultimately logical system, totally intolerant of interpretation. I think these ideas merit further development—after all, I haven't even begun to think about zero.

COMMENT:

Good essay in that it demonstrates the mind/thoughts of the author. The structure is well developed and the leading up to and conclusion of and going from cummings' poem is good style. Having the ending open is also a good idea—it shows that the thought process of this person is alive and still functioning. (HDT)

The logic is wonderful. So is the citing of e.e. cummings. The originality is superb. (PLF)

Annelise Goldberg
College: Yale University

PERSONAL STATEMENT

At the age of four the fact that I would one day fall from the platform into the tracks below seemed beyond question. The only point which needed further clarification was the exact distance that there would be between the oncoming subway train and me. While keeping a firm grip on my mother's hand, I thought about my various escape options, for certainly I had no intention of letting the train triumph. The first escape route to be considered was my mother and so, cocking my mary-janed foot to one side, I gazed up appraisingly; was speedy action, saving her youngest child, and only daughter, from the snarling teeth of the train, one of her many virtues? Much as I loved my mother, I thought not—she was much better at reading stories.

Ah, well, if my mother wasn't going to save me then I'd have to think of something else. Still attached, I ventured a brave toe to the yellow line and, holding my breath, peered down into the tracks. Underneath the platform was a very shallow cavity. Pulling in my stomach, I concluded that a person as small as me might, if she tried very hard, be able to stow herself safely in this alcove until the train had passed. After I was very sure that the train really had passed and wasn't just lurking close by but out of sight to trick me, I would venture out of hiding, looking brave—a Hero. Heroes, I thought, invariable liked Chiclets. Certainly my mother, wishing to reward me for my great presence of mind, would shower me with Chiclets of every flavor imaginable. Of course, being a Hero, I would only eat them one box at a time.

All of this planning had made me hungry for Chiclets. Glancing up and down the platform, I spied a Chiclet machine and asked for a penny, which was given to me. The next problem that I had was that of choosing a flavor. Settling on Tutti-Frutti, I carefully put my penny in the proper slot and got a small pink box containing two Chiclets.

The chasm which I would have to cross in order to board the train seemed big and black—perhaps I would fall through. My mother said that she didn't think so but still I lingered; I felt pleased with where I was and thought that perhaps it would be all for the best if I stayed with my Chiclet machine. I hadn't figured the chasm into my escape plans. But my mother was stepping aboard and, just to keep track of her, I decided to go along, my mother being one of my more valued possessions.

Once aboard I totally forgot about the train's sinister side and became fascinated with the other people in the car. One lady had purple shoes and a fake leopard skin vest on. Another had a hat with artificial fruit on top. A man slept, snoring, and another man was picking his nose. Where were *they* going? I stretched and my feet almost touched the floor . . . soon I'd be grown up.

After counting the number of red shoes in the car I got bored and went to look out the back window at all the tracks that we were leaving behind us.

At that time subways were connected with Chiclets, shopping for winter coats, trips to the Central Park Zoo, and my mother's job. I liked the idea of having a job and hoped that I'd get one that was fun, like being a zookeeper. (How did the zookeeper get in the cage without the lions getting out? How many baby aspirins does a sick walrus eat?)

Later on I discovered that some of my friends came to school on the subway. For me, school and the dentist were both in bus territory. People on the buses were different and not as many of them slept.

More time passed and I found myself going to dance classes on the subway. My parents split and my brother and I became experts on the West Side line. At least three times a week I'd ride on the subway en route to my father's house. Waiting for the train I'd marvel at the once beautiful mosaics, now caked with dirt, that lined the walls. Once New York had been very proud of its subway system. This made me feel sad. Beggars would come through the cars and Wall Street executives would board the train, going home after a "hard day at the office." I became skilled at reading the newspaper over other people's shoulders and discovered that the numbers accompanying graffiti names referred to the streets that the artists lived on. Sometimes someone would strike me as interesting, or sad. Often people looked as if they were thinking hard. On some trips I thought hard and on others I read the posters and faces. Sometimes I slept and my fear of falling between the platform and the train lessened as I grew larger. However, the empty tracks still looked ominous and I retained healthy respect for the yellow line. Gradually, I started to cross chasms alone. I had heard that if you took a pee on the third rail you'd be electrocuted. I wondered what I'd do if I saw a hundred dollar bill lying in the tracks.

Going to a friend's house in Chinatown I would take the Lexington Avenue line and get off at Worth Street, a station which is housed in a Romanesque building. Wondering when the building had been erected, I gazed up at numerals which I was unable to decipher. Finally I came into the knowledge that x is not only the last letter of lox but also the numeral ten.

Often, I pretend that I'm someone else when I ride the subway. Sometimes people talk to you or you to them and sometimes you just stare at each other, each feeling that you are absorbing the other's soul.

On the way home from Sloan-Kettering the apparent normalcy of the subway and its passengers soothes me. I have just seen the cells and face of a girl no older than I who is dying of cancer. Would I be able to work with terminally ill people every day?

My blood boils when my ass is pinched. When I get off at the recently retiled 49th Street station, on my way to Schirmer's for flute music, my stomach gives a funny turn and I feel protective toward my dirty mosaics.

When I read about Odysseus, I look around to see who resembles Poseidon. Othello once rode across the car from me. Last week, in response to a poster, I decided to leave my organs to medicine.

I look at the waterfall in a glossy advertisement for KOOL cigarettes which reminds me of the sea, keeper of my other loyalties. The beaches on Cape Cod are rather deserted in October. Only a few fishermen are out fishing from the shore at that time of year. In I plunged, clothes and all, remembering the summertime taste of salt water.

Once I tried to compute the number of hours that I had spent on the subway but got tired before finishing. I've seen a lot of things and people that I would never have encountered any other way. My background contains European Catholic and Jewish forbears and New England stepparents, but no "believers": It was the smudged foreheads on the subway that introduced me to Ash Wednesday.

I'm glad that I have grown up in New York, but I think that it's time for me to leave for a while, to live in other ways and in other places, even if I eventually wind up returning to this one. I'd like to stay somewhere else for long enough to lose the feeling, which I have had when travelling across the United States and on my brief visits to foreign countries, of being a foreigner in a foreign place.

Wandering through the Met, I can be a coatless child or a Bendel's lady. I value the feeling of uniqueness and the power to choose how I live, both of which my environment has nurtured as inalienable rights. Living amongst many people of different professions, viewpoints, and origins has exposed me to multiple insights and perspectives and made me realize that there are many Answers. All lifestyles and professions have their own depths of competences and responsibilities. I am looking for my own blend. Many options are attractive to me.

I look at things and wonder how and why they work. What are the intricacies, how is the effect achieved? With these questions forever in my mind I, like many others, seek an education.

The subway is a small-scale version of what I find exciting and special about New York City. I can ride it to go see Goyas or simply to watch the tracks that I'm leaving behind . . . I do both.

COMMENT:

What is remarkable here is her ability to string the beads of memory into a lovely necklace. She re-creates a child's perception of the subway and then takes the subway through the rest of her life. She takes a simple aspect of her life—riding the subway—and uses that to thread the beads into the necklace. (PT)

Colin Hamilton
College: Amherst College

LOOKING AT HILLS

It's mid-August, around 95 degrees in the shade. I'm tired, stiff, and riding my bike through Iowa. I'm not alone; there are nearly 9,000 people for company. Every year about this time, people gather from around the country to join in RAGBRI—the Des Moines Register's Annual Great Bike Ride Across Iowa. People with no experience with RAGBRI may be quick to ask the question why, for there are no rewards—none that can be pinned or shelved. But what I'm gaining is immeasurable. The bonds I'm forming with my friends will keep us together no matter where we may be taken in the upcoming years. I'm learning about the generosity of rural Iowans who feed and shelter us. And riding, sometimes eight hours a day, I'm learning to look at hills.

The American Heritage Dictionary sums up a hill as "a well-defined, naturally elevated area of land smaller than a mountain." That doesn't give them enough credit. Hills are as diverse as those who wish to conquer them, each hill posing a unique problem. Each hill makes the rider calculate his speed and endurance, to focus his mind on a strong approach. Each hill will force the rider to respect it.

Iowa's hills, in particular, are misunderstood. To believe the media would be to believe Iowa is one flat cornfield, occasionally graced with a pig or cow. Instead, the cows and pigs, which are frequent enough, stand on plenty of hills, rolling and mounded.

As we left the western border, we encountered short, steep hills which demanded a racing start so we could easily climb at least the first half. Then a struggle ensued while I hoped my momentum would carry me to the top. More often, I was left inching up the final yards.

East of Eldora, we faced curved hills, on which I could never see if I was at the beginning or the end. On these I had to constantly adjust my speed to respond to the terrain, conserving my energy in case I was suddenly struck with a sharp incline with no chance for a running start. But I also wanted to maintain an intense pace because ahead lay rest, drinks, food, and showers.

Eventually these hills softened into long, mild inclinations which dragged on for a mile or more. In the beginning, the inexperienced rider, like myself, welcomed these hills, anticipating no rushing, imminent challenge. Before long though, I respected their ability to sap my strength. On the third and fourth days of the ride, it was far more common to see people walking these hills than the steep ones which we topped in only a minute.

Maybe more frightening than any hill is its antithesis: the decline. Rushing down a slope at 30 miles an hour with only two thin, floppy strips of rubber between me and a serious accident gave me a perspective far more real than any dictionary definition. On these slopes balance is everything, but at such high, unsteady speeds so little of it remains I could barely risk my head to see what I was riding from; I could only look dead ahead to where I was riding to, very quickly.

Occasionally, as we pedaled across the state, we met a hill which could be seen from miles away, looming menacingly, glaring down at us even as we crested the surrounding hills. These are the hills that festered in our minds, always influencing our conservation of energy and the planning of our rests. I learned to establish an equilibrium between preparation for these hills and putting them out of my mind. If I became too obsessed with them, I lost my concentration and with it my ability to conquer the smaller hills. But if I ignored the monstrous hills until I was suddenly on one, I was mentally and physically unprepared for the challenge. Sometimes the hill was more gentle than expected, other times far worse. And sometimes, as I approached, the path turned to the right or left and I'd be on the next stretch.

It is now December and I'm standing at the base of what appears to be a formidable hill, one which has dominated my horizons for a long time. The road into it seems to head east, but it is curved and I can't tell how far it will take me. There are many paths which would allow me to turn off, but they too are curved and hilly, although they may appear at first to be flat.

This is a hill almost all my friends have come to. Some have chosen to turn off; many are struggling with it now; many are forced to walk. Some will turn back and others, through hard work, preparation, and skill, will climb to the top where the views are good and there are endless roads to choose from.

I know it will be tough, but I have a running start and am usually a strong rider.

COMMENTS:

At first glance, long, but I was fascinated with this wonderful ability to bring the reader along. Colin has a real ability in written expression, and even though lengthy the essay works well. (JLM)

Long. A bit tedious in the telling, but a clever idea; a unique way to reveal Iowa, biking, and the author's approach to life and future goals. Seems worked on, fabricated, rather than spontaneously, naturally creative language. But good. (MAH)

Alan P. Isaac
College: Williams College

PERSONAL STATEMENT: RUMORS OF INNOCENCE

STAGE: Lighting is dim. Soft spotlights on characters onstage. The two characters, racially indistinguishable, sit on a church pew downstage center. Upstage is completely dark.

B: Does it hurt?
A: Not anymore. Not too much, at least.

B: It's sad, isn't it?

A: Not really, but once in a while, I would get snatches of memory, then a pang would suddenly surface from some well inside, cause a splash, then quietly die down.

B: Any regrets?

A: No, just second thoughts.

B: But, how do you feel? What do you do?

A: I sigh, then go with the next task.

B: It's not so bad, is it? I suppose every turning point makes you the person that you are. The self is formed this way, the mundane experiences are nothing more than the self expressing itself. But, really now, how much time do those turning points take when you put them all together?

A: No, we can't stop too long for anything . . . But innocence is so hard to sacrifice without some regret.

B: Everything we choose to make holy was never ours in the first place. Time comes when we have to give it up.

A: I suppose . . . I often wonder: What is there after innocence?

B: (*Pauses to think*) Why, . . . I guess, your whole life.

A: It was so safe in that bubble. When I was a child, in church I used to look up at the ceiling and stare at the lights up there. Each light was surrounded by all sorts of colors. They were all so pretty, I thought. I picked the three biggest and prettiest. They were Jesus, Mary, and Joseph. They were all up there protecting me. I was happy they did.

B: So, are they still up there?

A: I found out that it was just my eyesight failing me at such a young age. I needed glasses, that's all. It was my body's promise to gradually waste away. It was a nice thought, anyway. I still take off my glasses to see them now and then. (*Looks up.*) They look different now.

B: Are you still a Catholic?

A: (*Smiles.*) Yes? No? In my sense, yes. In my parents' pre-Vatican Two sense, no. But I found that Catholicism was one way. You can't follow The Way if the self is not filled with it. Each person has to find his or her way.

B: A way to what?

A: (*Pauses.*) I don't know . . . Salvation?

B: If there's no salvation? What then?

A: (*Pauses*) Well, . . . I guess there's nothing left but compassion . . . and God, maybe?

B: You still believe in God?

A: Yes, but I had to kill God before I could even begin to believe in a god. Empty myself of Him. What was left was . . . me. I had to realize myself first before God, since God will always be. I, on the other hand, will not. I have time, nothing else. Remember? We had to kill Christ first to gain eternal life.

B: But against God, don't you feel insignificant?

A: But, I don't hold myself against God, but with God. I don't try to objectify a deity. I don't make a box to deposit all my morals in.

B: How was it when you killed God?

A: Frightening. It wasn't God that I killed, though, but an idea of a god. I had to break that idol like I had to break the world my heritage had built for me and around me. One time my mother and I were having an argument. In the middle of it, she demanded: When are you going to start thinking and acting like a Filipino? I thought that a better question to ask was: When am I going to start thinking and acting? You see, I didn't want a world that was built for me, but a world built by me.

B: It's pretty scary out there. What do we have?

A: Choice.

B: Control.

A: Dreams.

B: Compassion.

A: And when all else fails, try dignity. It works sometimes.

(*Silence.*)

Are you finished praying?

B: I don't think I've ever stopped. How about you? Does it still hurt?
A: No. Not too much.
B: So, . . . what is left after innocence?
A: Why, your whole life.
   *(They look at each other, rise from the pew. They slowly part still
   looking at each other as
   Lights fade.)*

COMMENTS:

An excellent, rather unique portrayal of this student's philosophical and religious views. It is a bit risky—as essays for college admission go—certainly not standard. At times, it seems too narrow; at other times, too abstract. Actually it is probably both. The essay reveals a very clever, perceptive, mature author. (TG)

A creative, powerful essay—a beautiful handling of the "loss of innocence" or "quest for independence" theme. Another common subject matter presented in a crisp, clear, individual manner. (JWM)

Ameen Jan
College: Princeton University

THE TRAMP

The river is cold as fall changes to winter, and its water glides softly over the sharp rocks on the bed. The bank on both sides is pebbled, and further up gets forested with willows; the leaves have turned through orange and red to brown at this time of year, and each minute adds to the collection of these on the ground underneath. Chill winds blow in the early morning, when the sun is not strong enough to break through the clouds, and a light drizzle starts to fall on the downy leaves up the bank. Soon droplets begin to form on the leaves still attached to their boughs, and as they collect, the foliage starts drooping lower until the accumulated water drops off the ledge.

The tramp gets up at this time, for his face is cold. He quickly gathers his meager belongings in the bundle of tattered clothes that he carries with him, and makes his way to the bank of the river. He quickly rinses his face with a handful of water, for it is freezing cold, and runs his fingers through his matted hair (or at least makes an attempt of it). The morning ablutions are done.

Under a spreading willow, which still retains some of its foliage, a few yards up the river he seeks temporary shelter. He reaches into his coat pocket and draws a half-eaten can of beans and a bent spoon. He crumples the lid over with the utmost care, for its edges are sharp, and reaches into its contents. The congealed mass of food is slowly dislodged from the sides of the can, and the tramp starts to chew on the cold morsels.

The end of morning meal signifies the start of a day-long trek upriver to the town. Perhaps he can get a job there, maybe as a laborer, for the harvest is over and so is his last job as a picker at a farm. He would wake up early if he had a warm bed to sleep in and a roof over his head; he would work hard all day, laying bricks or carrying luggage at the railway station or running errands for a store. He would work hard if he could get a proper meal at a proper time, and have a routine set for him. Maybe he could even have a few friends, others like him roaming the country in search for jobs, and landing the same employment. He could progress, if given the chance, and prove his worth to the world . . .

By around noon the sun breaks through the clouds and the drizzle stops; the wet leaves and the soggy ground start to dry, and the atmosphere assumes a slight degree of warmth. The leaves on the ground start to scatter as they dry, for the tramp's shuffling footsteps dislodge them from their bed. The river sparkles up ahead as the sunlight is reflected off its surface, but underneath it is cold and forbidding. There is nothing to be seen in the distance, but for the naked willows and the interminable river.

COMMENTS:

An excellent essay if descriptive writing is the object. The essay is especially good as it conveys the thought that this situation will continue as it is—as does the river—the use of nature as a dominant element in this essay is effective. Enough of the tramp carries arrows to get the idea—and nature and its continuance dominate the mood and thought of the tale. (DT)

The description of the physical surroundings is great, but the direction of the narrative is fuzzy, leaving a sense of confusion. (PLF)

Anne M. Knott
College: Yale University

TEN WAYS TO CELEBRATE LIFE

Set aside the homework long enough to go outside and smell the sweet springtime and see how blue the sky can be.

Take a walk in the greening woods and fields, make boats to float down the swollen creek, and listen to the birds singing.

Sit with a friend in a restaurant booth and order a chocolate milkshake with two straws.

Go to the arboretum and run through the woods and meadows until you collapse, climb trees, sing, roll down hills until you are dizzy, and let loose all that pent-up energy.

With the sun beating overhead, dive down down down into the clear cold lake and come back up slowly through the fractured sunlight.

Sleep out on a summer's night and count shooting stars and constellations. Wonder at life so small in a universe so big.

On a crisp fall day, go with many friends to roam the apple orchard, climbing trees and finding the biggest and best apples, tasting them all, and afterward of course getting fresh hot cinnamon doughnuts and cider.

Put on all the warmest clothes (not forgetting boots and mittens) and venture out with friends into the swirling blizzard to build a snowman and tackle each other in the snow.

Come in all ruddy-cheeked, put on warm dry clothes that are too big for you, and curl up by the fire with popcorn and hot cocoa while the snow melts on the kitchen floor.

Crunch through the snow with frosty toes caroling with friends, make sugar cookies, smell the evergreen, keep secrets, and sing out the Christmas cheer.

COMMENT:

I want to really like this essay answer of Anne's, but am not sure that her attempt works that well. The person she is indirectly describing here (i.e., Anne herself) is probably a warm, sensitive young woman who does indeed have a special zest for living; but we aren't convinced of that because the message of this "poetry in prose" is rather detached from a description of self. I suppose as a reader (and maybe an all-too-cynical one), I'd find myself asking, "Is she 'for real'?" If the essay question had asked the applicant how to best celebrate life, the answer would be a truly marvelous one. (RJO)

Zoe Mulford
College: Harvard University

Belgians grow in circles
like mushrooms in the rain.
Looking down from a window
on a schoolyard at recess
the girls appear in little rings
like a yeast colony—
conversational huddles
that grow and regroup
and divide like cells.
To enter a circle
you go around and kiss each person
even the ones you don't know.
Always kiss
        hello goodbye goodmorning goodnight.
As cheek brushes cheek
you verify
        I am a person
        You are a person
        We have a basis for communication.

It took me a while to catch on,
coming from a world of determined individuals
who disdained cliques,
studied at the lunch table,
looked up suspiciously
if you said good morning.
Here the girls thought I was standoffish
when I only said it once.
My host-mother shook her head.
        Well, she's an artist.
        Her mind is elsewhere.
        She's ignoring us.
Now I kiss
        hello goodbye goodmorning goodnight.
Cheek brushes cheek.

I ask "ça va?"
really wanting to know.
I learn people's names
who they're related to and how,
what they've been doing.
In a room cold with grief
the family circle gathers to kiss for the last time
an uncle dead of leukemia.
Women weep together.
I stand bewildered with the close relatives
as all I can offer is respectful silence
filling a space in the ring.
In a room warm with birth
they gather to kiss for the first time
a long-awaited nephew.
I smile and coo with the rest
and study this new little foreigner
who will learn
as I am learning
by watching.

In kitchens full of soup-smells
where the steam from the pressure-cooker
condenses on the windows
and November's nasal-drip
spatters on the red roofs.
Circles of old women gather for coffee
to talk birth and death and weather
mothers and daughters and women's work,
and I sit with them listening
and asking questions.
I piece together the cycles,
marking the place I would fit in
were I not flying away again in July.
Letters from my mother
talk of adapting the tribe for modern life,
forming supra-family neighborhood support networks.
I am taking notes for her.

Circles can strangle
as well as protecting.
They've burned witches here.
Strong women have been broken over the dishpan,
noble men stifled in the mines.

Kristen Mulvihill
College: Brown University

CONFIRMATION (FAITH JOURNEY?)

All of the other little angels were wearing white. Why wasn't I?

To be honest, it didn't much concern me. I felt I was worthy of the color; however, it was not symbolic pageantry that mattered, but rather good intention. Who ever said white made one holy? Besides, it *was* past Labor Day and I didn't want to commit a "sin" in the name of the Father, the Son, or the Holy Spirit.

You may have surmised by now that I am entering into a realm, sometimes better left untouched, as I reflect upon an event, which although performed with good intention, served only to overshadow the true significance of the occasion, as well as to challenge my personal beliefs.

I remember Confirmation. How could I ever forget it: the long ceremony, the dignified bishop, the parishioners at their holiest.

But what was most important on that auspicious occasion was the true meaning of Confirmation, the "for what" and "for whom" it was intended. As to just what the exact purpose was, I am still pondering. However, as to "for whom" it was meant, the answer is as clear to me today as it was then: for the parents, of course, and for the Church that took the opportunity to show its holiness and to demonstrate humility.

For the parents, it was a sign of hope. The mothers were so proud, their eyes filled with tears of joy. And why not? Each of their daughters were wearing white, a color most suitable for their sixteen- and seventeen-year-old "innocent girls." The fathers were also elated. For many of them it was a first: "the first Sunday Mass in seventeen years." It was, too, a chance to rename their sons, to give them holy titles other than doctor or counselor. They were so proud of *their* sons——so proud in fact, it's a wonder none of them chose the name Jesus for their son. Then again, humility is a characteristic common to all good Christians.

This humility was best exhibited by the bishop, God bless him, who wore a large ring, which he, out of graciousness, permitted all to kiss. He wore a robe, laden with gold. However, it too was quite modest, as it had no waistline and was anything but revealing. He brought with him an assistant, a middle-aged, rather handsome priest. Looks did not go to his head either, as he was sure to smile at each female candidate as she approached the altar. He too was most humble. Upon numerous occasions, he helped the bishop straighten his foot-tall crown, handed him his long gold staff, and generally did anything his excellency requested, as long as he could look holy doing it. Undoubtedly, he eagerly awaited the day when, after the requisite period of study in Rome, he could fully relieve his excellency of his duties and assume the role of imparting the Holy Spirit into another generation.

The highlight of the event was the bishop's address, his words of divine advice to the "children" of our parish. It was indeed a speech I will never forget or forgive. He was especially kind to the female candidates as he spoke of "*the* grand future" ahead of us, of which he seemed to feel we were most worthy—"the vocation of wifedom and motherhood," as he so graciously phrased it. Deeply moved by this statement, I noted, with not too little irony, that chauvinistic stability that has characterized Holy "Mother" Church since the days of Peter and Paul. Isn't it nice to know some things never change.

The male candidates, of course, fully appreciated the speech. They seemed to be completely relaxed, brought to such a deep state of religious contemplation that they closed their eyes in silent, sleepy meditation.

Perhaps the parents related to the speech best of all, as they had experienced all of the self-fulfilling, religious experiences of which his excellency spoke: marriage, penance, and naturally planned parenthood.

Yes, Confirmation was for me a "true awakening." I regret to say it was neither what I expected nor desired.

Ironically, it contradicted rather than reinforced the values taught to me in Confirmation class. Yet, somehow, the disappointment of that day has taught me to rely upon my own beliefs. It has caused me to appreciate further the difference between the shallowness of pompous pageantry and the depth of simple ceremony.

COMMENT:

She hits much too hard at times (such as in criticizing the priest for smiling), but overall the essay succeeds because it brings out her personality. She takes quite a chance in writing this essay, but one which I believe is worth taking. This is a person I would like to meet.

This is a rare example of a cynical or sarcastic essay that succeeds as a college application essay.

James P. O'Rourke
College: Harvard College

PERSONAL STATEMENT

"Is this a high school or a museum?" I wondered. I had just walked through the doors of Regis High School and formed my first impression of the institution. The impersonal hallways and stone staircases gave me a cold feeling of insignificance. The sounds of the city outside came in through the walls and I realized I hadn't just chosen a school to attend—I had changed my way of life. Gone was my placid grammar school, set in the midst of acres of rolling Pennsylvania farmland. I would only continue to eat and sleep in my relaxed town of Titusville, New Jersey. My daily reality would now be a hurried four-and-a-half-hour commute to and from Manhattan, and the rigorous demands of an intense curriculum.

Almost four years later, I emerged from the daydreaming en route to Manhattan, amused at my freshman misgivings. The 6:59 express train had just departed from Princeton Junction, New Jersey. On board, I took in the familiar surroundings. Like every other day, the commuters had jammed through the doors to get seats for the long ride. After folding raincoats and stowing briefcases, the commuters settled themselves with their newspapers.

I too settled into my seat and reviewed my Classical Political Thought assignment. I began to read Plato's *Republic*. I was fascinated by Plato's ideas. He masterfully expressed much of what I found or suspected to be true in life. I read over the section on the education of the philosopher-ruler. Plato was so right . . . dialectic and rational discussion will always be important for those who want perspective and truth. But how many people share Plato's view in life? How many commit to the same priorities?

I sat there feeling something between despondency and frustration. Perspective was vitally important to me, and the challenge of communicating it to those seated around me seemed impossible. My mind began to shift from the analytical to the imaginative. I began to fantasize that the time had finally come to share my philosophy of life.

I imagined turning to my right. My first partner in enlightenment would be the kind-looking, middle-aged commuter seated next to me. I would begin confidently, picturing myself as Socrates questioning Cephalus or Thrasymachus.

"Do you know there are 130 people in this car . . . most of whom sit merely a few feet away from us. We sit next to these people every day. Do you realize that Plato—one of the greatest thinkers of all time—believed that dialectic could eventually lead people to the discovery of ultimate reality . . . The Good. Through the virtues of wisdom, justice, and discipline we attain knowledge of this Good. It, the Good, then permeates one's entire life, enabling him to do everything better. His whole person with all his faculties are raised to a higher level. If all this can happen through rational discussion of significant ideas among men, can you imagine the enlightenment potential just sitting in this one car? We could all be so much better off if we only conversed with each other on important issues."

I had made my pitch, I had taken my risk and shared with this decent-looking fellow what was important to me. Plato would have been proud. I awaited his reaction and response with eager anticipation as I studied his facial expressions. He looked at me quizzically, quickly but politely excused himself, stood up, grabbed his raincoat, and left the car. He did though continue to look back over his shoulder.

I came back to reality. The decent-looking commuter was still seated beside me, now showing signs of an impending morning nap. No damage done, but no meaningful communication effected in reality.

COMMENTS:

I would give this student an "A" if I were grading this as an English composition. It is cleverly conceived and well written. It wouldn't impress me, however, as an admissions tool in that it fails to reveal much about the author. (TG)

A "catchy" opening that immediately draws the reader into the life of Jim O'Rourke. References to Plato could have come off as forced and pseudo-intellectual, but the clear descriptions of the train and daydreams pull it into a well-written essay revealing an inquisitive mind. (JWM)

ESSAYS ON WORK
EXPERIENCE

Janet Dix
College: Brown University

"So, you have no previous work experience?"

"Nooo . . ."

"And this would be your first job?"

"Yesss . . ."

"Great, you can start Monday! I'll call you sometime during the week with hours. By the way, Janet, my name's Stephen."

All I could think was, but doesn't it say "Etienne" on his name tag? I couldn't believe that after wandering around the mall for 45 minutes, I had a job. Friends had told me job-hunting horror stories about applying at Christmastime and being turned down for the summer. Amazingly enough, 12 hours into the summer, the day after my last exam, there was a job.

Now, I'm not sure what my original picture of a Barnes & Noble employee looked like, but the difference between it and my current picture is comparable to the difference between a Van Gogh sky and a Bloom County comic strip. There are a collection of people whom I, under normal circumstances, would never have encountered, but now, after only a short while, I'm not sure I could get along without. Together, we teeter the line between truly bizarre and just plain entertaining. When Stephen explained to me that he shaves his legs because it cuts down on wind resistance while cycling, you could have heard a cotton ball hit the carpet in the store. Several of the more insecure males made a beeline for the door.

I imagine WORK, in capital gothic lettering, to be a sentence to be faced; a grim milestone to remind me that childhood was gone, and I now stood before a concrete wall of RESPONSIBILITY, also in capital gothic lettering. After all, my father goes to WORK every day, and his favorite clothing color is dark gray. His second favorite clothing color is gray. I figured that once I walked through the doors of Barnes & Noble, I would shed my trappings and suits of youth and become mature. I couldn't have been more wrong.

At Barnes & Noble, languid days are spent taking "vertical naps" on the extension ladder, or planning book cart relay races. Rearranging the "whale" is a favorite pastime, especially good for Friday nights, because every book from the huge central display must be moved to the floor directly in front of the door. This maneuver effectively blocks the door, and prevents customers from coming in and ruining our fun.

However, customers do manage to call, and they are quickly classified. Easy phone calls are highly anticipated, seldom received. "What time are you open 'til," is a favorite. A hard phone call is much more challenging:

"Last month, my cousin from South Dakota was in, and he said that halfway down on the left wall was a stack of pink books, and next to the stack of pink books was a yellow book with blue writing. Well. I want the one across the aisle from that!"

An equally challenging but more simply worded phone question: "I'm looking for a book." Long pregnant pause here. It's almost as if they expect you to tell them that Barnes & Noble is now selling natural vitamins instead of books. One has to reassure them. "I don't know the title, but the third letter in the author's name is X."

Those customers who sneak by our clever road block are classified also. An easy customer buys a book and has a bill totaling $3.76. He hands me $4.00 and apologizes because he doesn't have a penny. On the way, he actually picks up a book that he didn't even knock off the shelf.

A difficult customer selects $700.00 worth of books. Each book has all or part of its price sticker missing. Near the bottom of the pile he discovers a sodden piece of wood pulp that his daughter has chewed on. It used to be a book, and now he doesn't want it anymore. He attempts to pay with a MasterCard that has exceeded its credit limit. "Call for verification" flashes across the machine's screen. At this point, demonstrating some sort of herding instinct, all the customers in the store lumber up to the register like frightened wildebeest, ready to pay. Within seconds, all of them, including the original difficult customer, are clamoring and threatening to tell the manager of the terrible service. The manager, who has gone to the deli for a snack, walks up to the window, thinks better of coming in, and keeps walking as if he works in the video store next door.

Where could you go for an entree of books with a side order of comedy? Where could the management of a store operate like a five-wheeled vehicle and still survive? Where you can find me even when I'm not working? Barnes & Noble, of course, of course!

COMMENTS:

Janet manages to invest in the Barnes and Noble microcosm while sharing her worldview. That latter is funny, irreverent, and at times transcendent (as Van Gogh sky). Some of her narrative is a little forced; one strongly suspects that the *real* Janet is as much future customer as mischievous clerk. In the end, however, she dismisses the myth of adversary and reveals the insight of a very able and viable young candidate. (SAB)

This is interesting and well written. It is written from experience in a humorous way. Any reader who has spent any time browsing in bookstores could identify with the incidents described and so would catch the interest of admissions people. (BPS)

Celia E. Rothenberg
College: Wellesley College

Detasseling, simply defined, is the removal of the tassel from a corn stalk so that pollinization of the plant can occur and hybrid seed corn can grow. Among midwestern high school students detasseling is infamous because it requires extremely long hours in the July heat, tolerance of "corn rash" and bugs, and a lot of physical strength. I signed up in response to a dare from someone who believed that I would not be able to last the full six weeks. Perhaps it was the growing recognition of my own strength, my pride in being one of the twelve detasslers (out of the original seventy) who were asked to work the entire detasseling season, or the antagonistic nature of the dare that propelled me through all six weeks, but what I learned from that experience has changed me as a person.

Detasseling helped me to look beyond the surface of people who are different kinds of achievers from those I encounter every day. Attending University High School, I have learned to respect academic accomplishments above other types of achievement. Yet many of my fellow detasselers had completely different sets of values and goals that I came to admire. Many of them were working in order to eat, or to buy essential books and supplies for school. Being singled out as a "brain" from the first day because of the stereotype the students held of students from my high school was difficult. Yet I earned the respect of my crew by working hard, and we developed a friendly working relationship.

My partner, Josh, told me that the money he was making from the summer would be his only money for the rest of the year and would enable him to finish high school; college for him was an impossibility. Yet he never lost his sense of humor. Walking the three-quarters of a mile down each row, he would "rap," "I don't like to pick this corn, but I'm still glad that I was born." He gave me a true sense of what it means to make the most out of very little.

Speaking little English and understanding even less, two Thai girls who detasseled that summer never complained; together they could outwork the strongest and most experienced of the detasslers. Their determination to adjust to new surroundings and to work hard earned the respect of all of us.

The dynamics of the crew reflected the responsibility most of the crew felt toward the job and the farmer whose corn we detasseled.

There were days when we stayed after dark working by flashlight to finish a field so that it would not have to be plowed under, which would have meant a significant monetary loss for the farmer as well as a waste of three acres of good corn. Only after we finished did I realize that we had worked since 5 A.M. Since detasseling, I have not been a part of a group that requires every member to be as responsible as each crew member had to be then.

While discovering the strengths of so many different kinds of people, I also discovered some of my own strengths. I discovered my ability to respond to physical as well as academic challenges. I realized that I am able to depend on my own inner resources. This discovery of my own physical strength and my ability to endure came as a revelation to me.

Learning to judge people by different standards carried over into the school year when I realized that I did not have a date to the Junior Prom. Not used to staying home, I considered my options and discovered someone who was also dateless. A gifted math student, PLATO programmer, and someone who always carried a calculator, he seemed to have little in common with me. Even so, I asked him to Prom. Detasseling proved to me that different types of people can learn from each other, and we did. A very special friendship evolved after Prom, perhaps partly because of our differences and partly because we had taken the time and effort to discover that beneath the surface we share many things in common.

The concept of detasseling and what it requires is understood by few; yet those who have experienced it share a special bond. After detasseling we did not see each other again as a group, but we parted with respect for one another. I left valuing new things about myself and other people. And I also won the dare.

COMMENTS:

The amazing thing about Rothenberg's detasseling essay is that it worked despite leaning on populist platitudes about the American

Dream. It works because it is beautifully organized and the argument proceeds in concrete portions. It works because the writer manages to stay within the actual experience instead of sugarcoating it. It works because the determination and sentience for the writer is real. (SAB)

This essay is very well written. Through a summer job, which some college students might regard as somewhat demeaning, this student shows ability to adapt and versatility so necessary to adjusting to college situations. The writer shows a willingness to work hard for what she wants and through this she learns much about herself and others she worked with. She demonstrates through these experiences her ability to adjust (adapt) to new experiences, ideas, and people when she gets to college. (BPS)

Mina Le
College: Harvard University

"Mice and dice and spice and—" "Rice!" "And rice and nice and—what's that?—yes, 'tice'—very good!"

This rhyming exercise sounds like gibberish out of context, but when I was helping 5- and 6-year-olds learn to read this summer at the community center, I had no time to be embarrassed at how I sounded as we worked on phonics and rhymes. "Lll . . . aww . . . ggg. Now blend them—lllawwggg. Log." It wasn't until I started teaching such basics that I realized how abstract reading is, how hard it must be for kids to learn to connect characters with sounds and with thoughts! I tried to make phonics more concrete by connecting it to their lives, by saying, for example: "There's someone at this table with the 'nnn' sound in the middle of their name—can you find out who it is?" At this challenge the kids only stared at me as though I'd suggested eating leaves off trees, and even little Johnny, whose N's I referred to, had no idea what I wanted.

Fortunately, a break from the frustration came at recess, when I gladly relived my elementary-school days in crossing balance beams, riding the pulley, and accepting the kids' invitations to join their games. A girl pulling on my arm for attention would become an excuse to sing "Ding-dong, ding-dong!" as though my arm were a bell rope; soon kids were circling around to watch, enjoying the show until I had to announce that the bell was broken from overuse. So entertaining them was easy enough; the hard part of recess was bringing myself to call the kids back inside, after seeing how much fun they were having at games like the roaring Dragon Tag.

Though all of the children who went through the reading class were great—how can little kids not be—my favorite was a cute first-grader named Grace, whose sweet, affectionate personality gave me a reason to come to work each summer morning. She chattered pleasantly and precociously and was eager to give me hugs or take my hand. No one would have guessed it, but young Grace also happened to have a life-threatening allergy which could flare up at virtually any time, requiring her to carry epinephrine, Benadryl, and an inhaler with her in a pouch purse everywhere she went. In the event that Grace had an attack, one would have to administer all three medicines and call 911, making haste because the epinephrine would only work for fifteen minutes. Even living on the brink of death this way, the six-year-old took her condition in remarkable stride, calmly reminding me to bring the blue pouch purse every time we went out for recess. I had to admire her endlessly positive attitude.

It seems that children in general are like that, naturally imbued with optimism and with a bounding energy for life I couldn't help but pick up. This summer's reading students touched me more than they knew, simply by accepting and loving me as I was; and I, in turn, echoed their joie de vivre, encouraged their kind hearts, and tried my best to help them learn. I can already see how fulfilling a life of helping other people is going to be.

COMMENT:

The problem with this essay is that it tells only what the writer did at her job—the actual tasks. It doesn't say anything meaningful about the writer's experience of this job, except in ways that work against her. In the first paragraph, she essentially reveals that her approach to phonics didn't succeed, making her as happy as the kids to "break from the frustration" and go outdoors at recess. Only one child gives her "a reason" to go to work each morning. In the end, the generalities and platitudes about how great it is to work with children don't ring true because of this disconnect between evidence and ideas. (MR)

Ariel Fox
College: Harvard University

She scrunches her nose as she approaches the board, shoulders tensing as she takes another mechanical step forward. She is one of the regulars at the pool, one of the younger ones who comes to swim before dinner. I feel my impatience growing as she tentatively places a toe on the edge of the diving board. Why doesn't she just dive? I would love to throw aside my rescue tube and jump into the pool, for it is exceedingly hot. All day the sweat has been dripping down my face, mixing with my sunscreen to create a thin film on my sunglasses. All day the blueness of the water has been tantalizing me, urging me to end this heat-induced suffering. I have wondered at frequent intervals why someone like me with an overactive imagination and an almost physical need for conversation would torture herself like this—watching unappealing and practically inanimate objects move in random trajectories around a container full of chemicals (which read dangerously high on the pH monitor this morning). Joe relieving himself in the water was the high point of the day.

With excitement like this and the knowledge that sunstroke is imminent, I find it difficult to understand how this girl, her green hand-me-down suit barely clinging to her meager frame, can resist the lure of the water. Like Alice peering into the looking glass, she fights the unknown. Had I been her, indecision may have seized me as well, but it would have hit before I climbed the ladder—as soon as I had touched the board I would not have dared (or desired) to turn back. Yet she still stands paralyzed with fear. Perhaps she needs to prepare, perhaps she has never hurtled through the air before, arms flailing and knees crooked. Or perhaps she is a perfectionist, unable to tolerate less than a streamlined entry with minimal splash. Maybe she's not concentrating on diving at all, but instead imagining herself to be a mermaid, her green suit extended into a long fin. Whatever her reasons, she isn't ready to go off the board.

As she falters back and forth, her feet moving to her mind's distant drumbeat, I want to tell her to get on with it, to stop thinking about it. The same drumbeat of internal indecision has pounded in my head, subsiding only after decisive action. I can no longer bear the pounding, for as a lifeguard, I have what many in today's hectic world would give their souls (or their BMWs) for: time to ponder. But self-evaluation has its limits. Unfortunately, I am still vaguely aware of the paradoxical fact that without pondering, I would have never reached this conclusion. Yet why did my mind stumble so? With each stumbling step, the diver risks missing the opportunity to act. What if I blow my whistle and she is still waiting? Yet if she rushes, something may go wrong. Will she forgive herself, if, due to some unforeseen whisper of wind, her left elbow is askew as she enters the water? Maybe the mermaid wants one last look at dry land before she consigns herself to fate. It is difficult to recognize when the time has come to act, for clarity comes with hindsight.

While I can then empathize with the green-suited diver who has now wrapped her toes around the edge of the board, it is difficult for me to watch her internal (or imaginary) struggle. Maybe the answers aren't always within, and outside intervention is needed (if only to save the sanity of lifeguards working their last shifts). I lift my whistle to my lips, hoping that it is the stimulus needed to set the girl in motion—be it tumbling through the air or hopping back down on the hard, dry pavement. Secretly, I am hoping for a splash.

COMMENT:

Anyone who has been a lifeguard can relate to the combination of whistle-twirling ennui and lengthy contemplative opportunities described in this essay. The writer's descriptive prose is engaging, and her whimsical poolside reflections make for an interesting read. Her references to Alice and the looking glass and the mermaid are well placed, but the reader might speculate if sustaining either metaphor could have given the essay more impact. The writer clearly sees beyond the usual prosaic decision points at the diving board, but she goes beyond her slightly verbose but important third paragraph to drive home a smart denouement in an imaginative, well-crafted conclusion. (RK)

ESSAYS ON EXPERIENCES ABROAD

Matthew Yglesias
College: Harvard University

DREAMS OF MY RUSSIAN SUMMER

According to the *Time Magazine*/Princeton Review publication *The Best College for You and How to Get In*, the number ten essay topic to avoid is "your trip abroad, unless truly noteworthy." I am, therefore, about to commit an act of stunning intellectual audacity and state that my trip to Russia was not only noteworthy, but college application essay-worthy.

My first trip abroad was not of particular note: I went to the Czech Republic and lived in the small town of Telc while doing community service and visited the cities of Prague, Vienna, and Cesky Krumlov. I loved the trip and it intensified my interest in the history and culture of Eastern Europe. There was, however, a small problem—my pursuit of this interest revealed that I had visited only the wealthiest and most beautiful section of an often unpleasant area of the world. Something had to be done—I decided to spend the summer of '98 in Russia.

I learned that American Field Services sponsored a summer home stay program with Russian families in Nizhny Novgorod, a city that had been called in *The Economist* "the Detroit of Russia." Here, I thought, I could find the real essence of Eastern Europe.

After a two-day stay in lovely Moscow, I met my host family in the distinctly unlovely Nizhny Novgorod. The Zhemchuzhnikois live in a gray apartment block off Great Bolshevik October Revolution Street. Large Dumpsters sit in the center of the building courtyards, filled with trash that has gone uncollected for five years. During the summer, the government saves money by turning off the city's hot water supply. Such things as supermarkets have not yet reached this city of three million people.

The Zhemchuzhnikois are small in stature, and my feet hung well over the edge of my bed. My host father, Andrei, an engineer, spoke no English but gave me the nickname "*yelefant*" (elephant) in reference to my habit of banging my head on the low doorways. I like to think the time we spent watching the World Cup together and making anguished facial expressions at each poor play resulted in some connection across the language barrier.

Tanya, my host mother, is a medical doctor who took advantage of her July vacation to (over) mother me. She enthusiastically exchanged Russian and English words with me and lovingly cooked meals of delicious (though slightly poisonous) mushrooms which were enjoyed by the whole family. In the evenings the entire family would often bond together over stomach cramps and badly dubbed episodes of *Dynasty*.

Katya, my 16-year-old host sister, is a serious student and a Girl Scout. Despite my diligent efforts to learn Russian from the *Pimsleur Method* tapes before starting my journey, I was extremely grateful for her English skills. She was my friend and guide during my stay in a city which featured many aspects of my life in New York City (apartments, mass transit, pigeons) while remaining totally strange.

We visited such tourist sights as there are in Nizhny (war memorials, Socialist Realist statues, damaged churches) and met with the city's mayor, who told me that he didn't see any problem with having a Communist Youth League Metro station six years after the disbanding of the Communist Youth League. I "hung out" with Katya and her friends, participating in the day-to-day life of Nizhny Novgorod. I met a colorful drunk who kept me well informed of his political views, notably "we must give nuclear weapons to Cuba," and "a blockade! A blockade of the Baltics is the only solution." During the overnight train ride back to Moscow, I shared a compartment with three Russian men, and when I offered to share my Pringles and pierogi, I was offered in turn to share in the smoked fish and vodka they had brought aboard.

When I returned to America, I brought with me much more than photographs of the great Russian tourist attractions—I made an intense emotional connection with a family thousands of miles away whose language I do not speak, made new friends, saw firsthand everyday life in a country now very much in the news, felt at home in a foreign city, and learned some basic Russian.

Capitalism has not brought prosperity to Russia, and the government's near-total control of the media has stifled democracy. Extremist solutions to the country's difficulties were widely expressed even before the present crisis, and it is only the Russian people's healthy skepticism toward all public figures that has prevented extremists from coalescing behind an effective leader. In his book *The Clash of Civilizations,* Samuel P. Huntington has argued that future relations between the West and other civilizations (like Russia) must always be antagonistic—it does not seem to me that this future is inevitable, but it is in many ways the one to which we appear to be heading.

In Russia, I was directly exposed to what I believe will be the most important issue of the early twenty-first century—will America's defeated cold war enemies join the West, like Germany after the second world war; or will they return worse than ever, like Germany after the first? "Truly noteworthy?" I hope so.

COMMENT:

Unfortunately, this essay falls into the very trap it sets for itself: the opening paragraph claims that what follows will be "an act of stunning intellectual audacity" in describing a trip that is "truly noteworthy." But, really, this trip isn't. Or at least the writer hasn't convinced us of this, but rather has offered a hodge-podge of well-known facts about contemporary Russian life. (It's difficult; the beds are small; mushrooms are often used in cooking.) The writer hangs out and visits different sites. So what? There's a brief effort toward the end to discuss Russian politics, but nothing previously discussed in the essay suggests the writer's conclusion about the inevitability of future clashes between the West and Russia. Reading this essay, it's easy to understand why college applicants are cautioned against writing about their trips abroad. (MR)

Olivia Hung
College: Harvard University

CHANGES IN MY VIEWPOINT

December 16, 1994, was the last day of school before winter break. It would be the last day I would spend at ISS (International School of Stockholm) and with Lily-Ann, my best friend. I had spent most of my middle school years living in Lidingö, Sweden. The next time I would start school would be in rainy California. I would move back just in time to complete my course selection sheet for high school and to witness the floods that occurred that winter. The time I spent in Sweden helped me to broaden my once-provincial view of the world and to gain self-confidence.

As I left my friends, memories came to me, memories that I would not easily forget. I got a perspective of diversity in Sweden that I would not have gotten if I had stayed in my ethnically diverse but culturally identical community. I first noticed diversity when I stepped into my sixth grade classroom at the local elementary school. Almost everyone in the room was twelve and had blond hair and blue eyes; I was ten and I had black hair and brown eyes. My classmates were nice to me, but I never felt I belonged with them. Starting seventh grade at ISS, I found an international flavor to the student body, which was a pleasant change from an all-white society. I remembered when I was in fifth grade none of us dared to show our individuality for fear of other kids' laughs and jeers. At ISS I noticed that nobody was laughed at, shunned, or criticized for being unique. Classmates dressed, ate, and studied the way they wanted. Along with Lily-Ann, there were some people I met that were unforgettable. Joris was one of them.

I met Joris, whom many considered to be a jerk, in seventh grade. I remember him not because he was a jerk but because he always made me work harder. At the beginning of the year, our math teacher Mr. Vass told us that we could independently work ahead if we wanted to. After a month, working ahead had turned into a competition; we were running a race to see who could finish first. I was barely ahead of Joris; one time he was ahead by two sections. Telling myself I had been slacking off, I started working with renewed energy. Fueled by the freedom given by Mr. Vass to me in determining my pace and the competition from Joris, I was well into Algebra II and matrices when winter break came.

Lily-Ann and I spent that last afternoon hanging out and buying gifts. We bought each other pens with our names engraved in them. We knew it was going to be a long time before we saw each other again. As we parted, Lily-Ann told me, "Promise me you'll write. I'll never forget the time we spent together." Those two years are unforgettable to me as well.

COMMENT:

This writer conveys strong ambiguous feelings about her middle school experience abroad, as she makes the ironic point that this homogeneous community was where she first encountered diversity. Without referring to the title, however, it's hard to tell where she wants to go with the essay. Given the importance of her friendship with Lily-Ann, one wonders why she doesn't focus more on that relationship; and the paragraph about Joris doesn't add anything significant, other than to describe anecdotally one way that she develops self-confidence. The concluding paragraph fails to pull together the various strands of the essay. While an interesting piece, it just doesn't really come together. (RK)

Whitney Lee
College: Harvard University

I cannot speak Spanish. It is a fact that becomes blatantly obvious whenever I visit my mother because she lives in Argentina, but before sophomore year, she lived in Puerto Rico. When I was a child, I went to Puerto Rico every summer. We lived in a *villa* on the grounds of the Westin Rio Mar and had family in the small town of Rio Grande. My lack of Spanish skills was met with a mixture of disdain and fascination at the fact that I was a "unilingual" American. Though I explained to them that I studied French, it did little to convince them.

After months of pleading for a vacation in a French-speaking country, we went to the Canadian province of Quebec. I was looking forward to the role-reversal; for once, I would be the bilingual traveler and my mother would be the "Ugly American." To my surprise, she transitioned almost seamlessly, using her broken French as a jumping off point to start conversations. In doing so, she met many people who were eager for a chance to converse in English with a native speaker.

Her ability to connect with others baffled me. I did not understand how she could relate to them so easily, that is until I went to Ghana. Though I worked during the day, I was able to spend quality time with the girls attending the Nsaba Diaspora School, a recently built single-sex school in a rural village. They were in the process of learning English and I cannot speak Twi (their language), but we connected immediately. They took me to their classes, showed me the village and worked math problems with me on a chalkboard so we could compare problem-solving methods.

What brought us together was a shared desire to relate to each other and to experience life from another viewpoint. What I took away from that experience was that language does not have to function as a barrier if both sides are willing to look past linguistic differences and acknowledge shared humanity.

COMMENT:

This essay adds a new twist to a familiar topic: lessons learned from one's mother. The writer incorporates youthful feelings of inadequacy when compared to her mother with the lessons she has learned during some of her travels. The setting jumps from Puerto Rico to Canada to Ghana without seeming disjointed or random. This essay starts on the subject of language skills, or lack thereof, and then moves on to how language can end up drawing people together. By beginning with speaking about her lack of Spanish skills, she opens the door to then tell the reader that she can, in fact, speak French and, more importantly, has traveled to Ghana on a public service mission. The writer ends the essay with an important realization that she made about language and the fact that language does not have to be a barrier between people. One of the main reasons why this essay is successful is that the writer shows the reader how she was able to turn a weakness into a strength. (AMH)

ESSAYS ON
WRITING

Anonymous

LITTLE BUGGY

It started, I guess, with that little buggy—really started, I mean, though the roots had been laid down almost since birth—in around the third grade. I could tool around in that thing, and when I was in it I was indestructible, and with a touch of a button (and there were always plenty of buttons) I could have anything from a pumpkin pie, no crust, to a super solar space modulator beam; and I could zip around, zip forward, zip backward, and I could zip up and down and through the water and in deepest space and through time and the dimensions.

I really liked that little car. I used to think about it as I drifted off to sleep. That was when the idea came to me: The floor beneath my bed would open, dropping me into a flowing crimson river; and as I traveled at breakneck speed toward certain doom, I would press a button and the bed would, yes, *change* into that little car.

So I wrote it down.

I wrote it during classes and after school and while I watched *The Six Million Dollar Man*. I started with the flowing river beneath my bed, and quickly graduated into my adventures against Mouse Man and Super Mouse and The Mouse that was Nasty. And after I beat the mice, I fought the men, like Owl Man and Evil Man and Nasty Man. Then I hit the really big time, in this little book, and fought people with names like The Black Shadow and Jim McCoy, agent of S.K.U.L.L.

And when fifth grade was over, I'd finished my first book. Eighty pages if it was a paragraph, was my book, written in careful letters on wide-ruled paper.

Then I started thinking. How to follow up my masterpiece? A friend and I were churning out "King Comics Corporation" at the rate of two or three comics a week . . . but these were simply excuses to draw two men hitting each other. I wanted a lot. I wanted realism. I wanted . . . what did I want?

I wanted to write a Choose Your Own Adventure book, and, come the end of the sixth grade, I had written two (one called *Great White* and the other oh-so-tentatively titled *The Presidential Factor*) and had gotten a friend to start working on publishing them for me. I didn't gross ten dollars, selling those things to classmates, even though the teachers let me Xerox them at half-price. Still, I was inspired. For my first "real" book.

It hit me at the end of tenth grade, after I had recently written enough short stories to fill two anthologies. I had just written a ninety-page story, and I thought: hey, Why not expand it?

So I started, and found out I didn't know what the hell "expand" meant. Was I meant to bloat it? Add extra characters?

So I started from scratch. The main character in my stories had always been an extension of what Stephen King calls the "I-guy." And, it seemed, I just wasn't strong enough as a personality to carry a book-length project. To keep a simple outline, I developed an idea that basically bracketed episodes. I wrote the start and the end in fifty good pages, then went back and began to fill it in.

As I went I sort of lost track of the gimmick of the novel, and it became loose and confusing. I finished, sent it to a contest, sent it to an agent, and was duly rejected. By both. It hurts a little, still, the little twinge at finding a one-page rejection, always with the finishing sentence: *I can tell you're a writer with promise.*

But here I am, working on my new masterpiece, with two good working titles and a main character that should allow for hundreds of pages of interesting revelation. It is *Brittle Leaves and Skeleton Trees,* sometimes called *Without Style or Grace;* and who knows? Maybe it'll be on the stands in not too long. And if it won't; well, there's more to come. Plenty more to come.

COMMENTS:

There is a pleasantly vibrant evocation of childhood imagination in this essay. There is also, at times, a kind of transparent respect for slickness. A writer need not advertise the *quantity* of writing but rather reveal its *quality* by what it stated. This essay wavers between the phantasmagoria of imagination and meretriciousness. (SAB)

This is good. It is interesting and well written. The person obviously has a talent for writing and the experiences demonstrate a persistence that will lead to success. We just might see something "on the stands" written by this person. (BPS)

Michael Chaskes
College: Wesleyan University

Why I Want to Be a Writer

I do almost all my writing in my bedroom. The prewriting I actually do in bed, lying down, with my eyes closed. That way, no one can tell if I'm asleep or just thinking. Sometimes when I do that I really do go to sleep, but that's part of it, you see.

While I sit and write, I look out the window. The blinds are venetian, and even when they're totally closed I can still see out of them. The blinds make big horizontal stripes over the sky, and as birds swoop down, they are continually obscured, then visible, then obscured, then visible. The birds land on branches; then sometimes I can see all of them clearly, but usually I see only part of them, and sometimes none of them.

When I get tired of writing, I pick up a book. I have a lot of them in my room. Then I'll read, or just stare at the cover. Sometimes my favorite part is the author's biographic sketch. In his, Woody Allen says that "his only regret in life is that he's not someone else." I don't find that funny at all.

Sometimes, I'll get a drink and a copy of the paper or *Newsweek*. *Newsweek* always depresses me. I think it's because they always think they know exactly what's going on, even when the people involved don't.

Or maybe that's not it. I don't know.

There's also an alarm clock in my room. I hate the clock almost as much as I hate the calendar. It only tells two kinds of time to me: "plenty of" and "almost out of." I think "plenty of" is worse because it's an illusion, and when I think I have "plenty of," I look back at the clock a little while later and I'm already "almost out of." I don't like the alarm too much either, it's too loud.

Well, maybe none of that tells you why I want to be a writer, but that's really it, or most of it. Or some of it. Sometimes I feel like the best place to do all my writing would be outside somewhere, by a lake in Maine or something, like an artist with an easel, my typewriter and I, all the time. But then it would rain, and all my work would get wet and ruined. So I just stay in my room. I have trouble seeing out of the window, but everybody has to make do, don't they?

COMMENT:

Michael's essay reminds me of Andy Rooney. He speaks of simple, everyday things in simple ways, but his observations are offbeat, refreshing, and honest. The best part of this essay is that it lets the reader into the private life and thoughts of the writer, into his personal self, just as Holden Caulfield did. It is totally fitting that the essay was handwritten and not typed, because of the unavoidable tone of formality that accompanies a "perfectly presented" piece. (AST)

Nikolas R. Elevitch
College: Yale University

I DO MANY THINGS, but there's no question that the most important to me is writing.

The other things I do I like for different reasons. I like running, for example, because it is a way for me to make noise physically and competitively. Writing is also venting, but it comes from the quiet voice, quiet breathing, and the loud mind.

I like playing in a rock band because that too is noisy. I can use my hands playing the bass guitar and work with Philip, the drummer. The drums and bass have to be tight, fit in a groove, be the pulse of the music. But what I like most is the way Philip and I build off each other. Philip might introduce a quick off-beat roll and lead into hitting the upbeats between the quarter notes. I have to adapt to this change, but at the same time, I follow through with a rapid walking line from 4/4 to 7/8. Philip keeps hitting those upbeats and the groove changes, the song rises to a new level, a new rhythm.

This partnership is not unique to a band. What brought out and developed my ability to write is a partnership I had with my friend Rob. We would have rap sessions in which the purpose was to create a continuous flow of laughs (keep the other guy laughing).

A good metaphor for our rap sessions is our first Ping-Pong game. Rob was about to serve the ball, but ended up serving a volley of images. He paused to help me imagine Ronald Reagan falling asleep on his desk and accidentally leaning on the red button. I said that the maid would come and ask what he wanted. (So much for the power and control of the President.) I then closed my eyes for no reason and snored, and he did too. We did this for a minute and then began something else. We would do this all the time, while eating, watching TV, etc. Actually there was rarely a serious moment. We constantly searched for things out of context to chuck into the buildup, things funny just because of the way they bounced off each other, weird and from the blue.

But when I want to do something all by myself the most important thing to do is write. Once accidentally I sat at a typewriter and played with words, chucking things on the page just for the sake of getting it out and feeling the keys go click, and out came a mixture of words built upon from one another. To my surprise, this first poem later went on to be published in the *Boston Literary Review*. It was so easy to get on paper the images floating around in my mind that I wrote many more poems throughout my junior year, getting three accepted for publication. The big obstacle for me had been getting these images to work well together. They played off the subconscious, each other, and the sounds of the words themselves.

I spend time alone writing in a room at the top of a building that I walk to at night with a flashlight. I can look out at the Hudson River, the lights on the other side, and the trees blowing in the darkness on my side. Out of the 200 scientists that work there, maybe one diehard remains, his lonely car in the parking lot. I close the door and sit at the typewriter and start:

My activity is mud wallowing.

To begin again:

I left home but didn't know where to go. I remember what my dad told me the night before, 'Son, you must get a mate.' I am an animal, I know that. But I was intent upon following the food supply, not a mate. Or at least my instinct. But not a mate. I am lonely and strange. Last night I did go straight to the fridge for a Coke, but I only did it because I rolled a 6-sided die and came up 3.5. Maybe I should just plop down here on the street and renounce everything, submitting myself to destiny. Someone will care for me. (I fell facedown in the mud, my pants leg catching a nail on the doorstep and ripping.) I submit myself to the street—*as it is*. Let myself be carried away with Main Street America. By the dice. My life might turn up all 3.5s, summed up in one word. Probability.

I stop. I realize that I'm going in circles. But I've uncovered something along the way. So all I can say is that when I write, I investigate ideas and feelings, my own and other people's. I bandy with the images in my brain and learn about, for example, my frustration with Main Street America, and the monotony of my walking toward destiny as it shows in real life through daily repetition. I fall in the mud. I even take on the world.

Carol Zall
College: Princeton University

The Essay. It is supposed to make me come alive as a person. Expressing my goals, values, and personal development would be helpful. In fact, the pamphlet I have just read on writing college essays gives me any easy tip: "Try for essays that provide insights into *all* these areas: 1) your intellectual and creative interests; 2) your personal strengths; 3) how well you write; 4) what's special about you." Sure. Right-o.

It is not that I find writing difficult. In fact, writing is one of my greatest pleasures, and has been ever since my poetic debut in the third grade with "O Frog." "Where do you get your croak?" I lamented. "Or your black-spotted cloak? Or black beady eyes? Or toenails that look like twisted bow ties?" Masterful, yes. But the point is, if I am provided with a subject, I will happily set pen to paper. However, assessing one's life can be rather tough.

Then there is the question of what to focus on. I could wax philosophical and give my views on the morality of war. But, I did that this summer in a letter to a friend and nearly killed the relationship. (I started casually enough: "Dear Bob, how are you? The weather here is just fine." Then I threw him the curve. "Just a few thoughts that were going through my mind—Is War Moral?" This was followed by a four-page dissertation on the subject.) Fine, forget the intellectualism. How about discussing the meaningful aspects of my experiences—the satisfaction that comes from tutoring, the new and different people whom I met while working at a "fast food joint" and the insight I gained from the experience (how to fill a straw holder, how much ice to put in the cup, how much a Whopper-without-the-meat costs), even the way I like to think while I ride my bicycle. But—no, it is all too mundane, the same meaningless "meaningful essay" which everyone will write.

Maybe the fact is that I think too much. My mind is constantly working, churning up ideas on an endless number of subjects. One day I can become artistic and take out my paints. Another, I ponder the implications of nuclear war and call a citizens' group to find out what I can do. There are so many things that interest me, so much in which I can find meaning, that it is impossible to choose one event and let that represent me. It is not that I lack direction—I do know my main area of interest—but rather that my outlook embraces all of life. To me, everything seems interconnected, bound together in one overwhelming network. There are no isolated disciplines, all knowledge is inextricably interwoven. And so, even if I think about physics one moment, and the meaning of life the next, and third-grade poems after that, they are all tied together by the common thread; they are all part of my exploration of life.

Nearing the end, I am wondering if the essay is not a little *too* unconventional. However, I like what it represents: a willingness to take risks, a regard for both humor and serious thought, an interest in life, and a certain confidence that living is always an adventure. Sounds like me.

COMMENT:

This essay falls into the trap of telling the reader what the writer wants him/her to conclude. "My mind is constantly working, churning up ideas on an endless number of subjects." "However, I like what it [the essay] represents: a willingness to take risks, a regard for both humor and serious thought, an interest in life, and a certain confidence . . ." The truly outstanding essays present such a compelling picture of the writer that there is no need to prompt the reader toward the desired conclusions to be drawn. (AST)